ADVANCE PRAISE FOR

Focus Groups: Culturally Responsive Approaches for Qualitative Inquiry and Program Evaluation

"Dr. Hall artfully demonstrates how to use culturally responsive focus groups for social justice through practical research techniques and case examples that show how the researcher can be an agent of change and give a voice to marginalized communities."

Stacy Penna, Ed.D.
NVivo Community Director
QSR International

Focus Groups

QUALITATIVE RESEARCH METHODOLOGIES: TRADITIONS, DESIGNS, AND PEDAGOGIES

Kathleen deMarrais; Melissa Freeman; Jori N. Hall; Kathy Roulston, *Editors*

The *Qualitative Research Methodologies: Traditions, Designs, and Pedagogies* series is designed to encourage qualitative researchers to look both backward and forward in the field of qualitative inquiry. We invite authors to submit proposals for both single-authored books and edited volumes focused on particular qualitative designs situated within their historical, theoretical, and disciplinary/cross disciplinary contexts. Pieces might include a tradition's or design's historical roots and key scholars, ways the approach has changed over time, as well as ethical and methodological considerations in the use of that particular research approach. They may also provide an introduction to contemporary designs created at the intersection of multiple, theoretical, and often assumed incommensurable historical paths. In addition, we encourage authors to submit proposals for books focused on the pedagogy of qualitative research methodologies that interrogate how we prepare researchers new to qualitative research methodologies with the theoretical, methodological, and ethical understandings and skills for their work.

BOOKS IN THE SERIES

Focus Groups: Culturally Responsive Approaches
for Qualitative Inquiry and Program Evaluation
by Jori N. Hall (2020)

Exploring the Archives:
A Beginners Guide for Qualitative Researchers
by Kathryn Roulston and Kathleen deMarrais (2021)

Those interested in being considered for inclusion in the series should send a prospectus (https://zfrmz.com/rmlvGq7xgL2RTgPkByk9), CV, and cover letter to:

Kathleen deMarrais
kathleen@uga.edu

Focus Groups

Culturally Responsive Approaches for Qualitative Inquiry and Program Evaluation

By Jori N. Hall

Myers Education Press

GORHAM, MAINE

Myers
Education
Press

Copyright © 2020 | Myers Education Press, LLC

Published by Myers Education Press, LLC
P.O. Box 424 Gorham, ME 04038

Myers Education Press is an academic publisher specializing in books, e-books, and digital content in the field of education. All of our books are subjected to a rigorous peer review process and produced in compliance with the standards of the Council on Library and Information Resources.

Library of Congress Cataloging-in-Publication Data available from Library of Congress.

13-digit ISBN 978-1-9755-0193-8 (paperback)
13-digit ISBN 978-1-9755-0192-1 (hard cover)
13-digit ISBN 978-1-9755-0194-5 (library networkable e-edition)
13-digit ISBN 978-1-9755-0195-2 (consumer e-edition)

Printed in the United States of America.

All first editions printed on acid-free paper that meets the American National Standards Institute Z39-48 standard.

Books published by Myers Education Press may be purchased at special quantity discount rates for groups, workshops, training organizations, and classroom usage. Please call our customer service department at 1-800-232-0223 for details.

Cover design by Teresa Lagrange.

Visit us on the web at www.myersedpress.com to browse our complete list of titles.

CONTENTS

Contents

ACKNOWLEDGMENTS

I would like to acknowledge my friends and family who supported me during the writing of this book. Your care throughout this process was invaluable. A special thanks to the PhD students, contributors and colleagues who provided thoughtful feedback, offered narrative accounts of culturally responsive focus groups in practice and advanced critical thinking on how to address social inequities through culturally responsive focus group inquiry. I am indebted to each of you.

A S THE WORLD BECOMES more diverse, it becomes increasingly imperative to conceptualize and utilize methods in ways that are responsive
to the uniqueness of participants and programs, as well as to a particular
research design. Accordingly, this book, *Focus Groups: Culturally Responsive Approaches for Qualitative Inquiry and Program Evaluation*, takes an
in-depth look at how to develop and implement culturally responsive focus
groups within the context of qualitative inquiry and program evaluation.
The purpose of this book is twofold: (1) advance a culturally responsive
stance that treats focus groups as sites of social justice and (2) showcase
how various forms of focus groups attend to the cultural contexts of prioritized communities as well as address inquiry goals. To support these purposes, practical guidance on focus groups and cross-disciplinary case examples
from culturally responsive researchers and evaluators are woven throughout
the book.

Chapter 1 sets the stage for the text, presenting foundational information, including the definition of focus groups, an articulation of the culturally responsive stance used to frame the book, and a brief historical review
of qualitative research and program evaluation.

Chapter 2 discusses key components of inquiry design, emphasizing
how inquiry components interact with each other and how the inquiry
components are intended to advance cultural responsiveness. Here I discuss
common design options or methodologies that are compatible with focus
groups, the appropriateness of focus groups for your design, and other important aspects of inquiry design such as participant sampling and recruitment. The chapter ends with a discussion of ethics, focusing on the role of
ethics committees, gatekeepers, and informed consent.

Chapter 3 begins with a discussion on how to develop a focus group
protocol and offers strategies to meaningfully engage focus group participants. Next, I turn my attention to describing the moderator role. I outline
the facilitation skills required to moderate a focus group and explicate the
role of the moderator as a research instrument and agent for change.

In Chapter 4, I offer readers multicultural validity and inquirer reflexivity as criteria for establishing focus group quality. I give a range of techniques and mechanisms for applying these criteria and ensuring design components are culturally congruent with participants' concerns. Finally, I present a case example to underscore some of the key points made in the chapter.

Chapter 5 examines pertinent aspects to consider when developing and implementing culturally responsive focus groups with youths and older adults. The case examples from evaluators featured in this chapter demonstrate how different culturally responsive techniques (i.e., strength-based theories, photo-elicitation) were applied to focus groups to address the linguistic diversity of youth participants and to accommodate the varying cognitive abilities of older adults.

Chapter 6 advances Indigenous- and feminist-oriented focus groups while recognizing the complexities inherent in the terms "Indigenous" and "feminist." I explore different perspectives on Indigenous- and feminist focus groups and give two case examples. The first case describes a non-Western focus group approach and the second presents a feminist-oriented focus group approach drawing on the concept of intersectionality.

Chapter 7 offers a brief review of online focus groups, highlighting two types: synchronous and asynchronous. The case example presented in this chapter underscores how synchronous focus groups are particularly responsive, as they permit geographical diversity and afford participant privacy and convenience.

In Chapter 8, I explain some approaches to support culturally responsive analysis and interpretation of focus group data. The chapter includes discussions on transcribing focus group data, nonverbal focus group communications, and how computers can assist with data analysis and interpretation. This chapter is designed to encourage thoughtful adoption or adaptation of the analytic strategies presented in order to generate credible cultural insights from the focus group data.

Overall, this book is intended to promote cultural sensitivity when designing focus groups. Ultimately, I hope the book encourages more attention to the culture and context within which a focus group is situated and motivates thoughtful and creative uses of focus groups as sites for social justice.

CHAPTER ONE

Introduction

In This Chapter

- What are Focus Groups?

- Focus Group Origins

- Overview of Qualitative Research and Program Evaluation

- Conceptual Strands Related to Cultural Responsiveness

- Contemporary Focus Group Use

- Bringing it All Together: My Stance on Culturally Responsive Focus Groups

IN THIS INTRODUCTORY CHAPTER, I provide a definition of focus group and a brief history of its origins. Next, I review qualitative research and program evaluation, the fields within which I work and the fields that serve as the disciplinary landscape for this book. I then trace conceptual strands of cultural responsiveness that are dominant in the education and evaluation literature, highlighting how I have come to understand culturally responsive practice. Considering the history of qualitative research, including focus groups, and previous articulations of cultural responsiveness, I end the chapter with my stance on cultural responsiveness, which I use to frame this book.

What are Focus Groups?

Focus groups are a qualitative research method designed to generate information about a specific topic through a group discussion (Krueger & Casey, 2015; Morgan, 2019; Patton, 2015; Ryan, Ganda, Culbertson, & Carlson, 2013). Priority questions asked by a researcher or evaluator serve to focus the group discussion and determine the type of information generated from the collective conversation (Ryan et al., 2013). Like individual interviews, focus groups aim to draw out and examine personal experiences, perceptions, and values. However, focus groups are distinguished from interviews in that they do not focus on one-on-one (interviewer and interviewee) interactions. Instead, a focus group aims to enable conversations among participants. This means the inquirer does not take center stage in the group discussion. Rather, the inquirer centers participants' experiences. Functioning in this capacity, the inquirer's role is that of a *moderator* or facilitator. In addition to facilitating a collective conversation, moderating includes observing participant dynamics (Massey, 2011). From this perspective, focus groups take on a bit of an anthropological lens in that they are used to collect data on, and understand, aspects of a group's culture. In this way, focus groups provide valuable cultural insights related to a group's language, behaviors, social practices, and activities. Yet, it should be noted that while focus groups include observational data, they are distinct from observations. For instance, observations commonly occur in people's natural settings and aim to capture spontaneous interactions and conversations. In contrast, focus groups are contrived. They are typically the result of an inquirer recruiting group participants, assembling the group in an agreed-upon location, and moderating the discussion.

The following sections further contextualize focus groups by reviewing the origins of focus groups and their link to qualitative research and program evaluation.

Focus Group Origins

Robert K. Merton's innovative work on the *focused interview* played a key role in the development of what we now call focus groups. Merton had been invited by Paul Lazarsfeld to work in the Bureau of Applied Social Research at Columbia University. Merton's focused interview was the result of working for several years at the Bureau to incorporate interviewing techniques into research on the psychological effects of World War II propaganda communications (radio, print, and film) (Merton & Kendell, 1946). Lazarsfeld, Merton and their colleagues considered the qualitative data from focused interviews useful to elaborate on the experimental studies they conducted at the Bureau. In addition, these researchers found focus groups valuable to: (a) provide insights on significant and unexpected aspects of an event, (b) understand the perspectives of subgroups in a population, (c) reveal differences between expected and actual effects, and (d) validate theories and other relevant literature used to guide studies (Merton & Kendall, 1946).

Despite the identified benefits of focus groups based on the empirical work conducted at the Bureau, focus groups were not enthusiastically taken up by academics or evaluators (Kidd & Parshall, 2000). A reason for this was the preoccupation within the social sciences with quantitative methodologies and methods (Kidd & Parshall, 2010). By the 1950s, however, and well into the 1970s, focus groups had become popular among market researchers to: (1) understand consumer satisfaction with services and products, (2) obtain perspectives on potential services and products, (3) evaluate advertising campaigns, and (4) develop questionnaires to further investigate advertising campaigns (Cox, Higginbotham & Burton, 1976). By the 1980s, qualitative research was in vogue, giving rise to focus group use among social science researchers and program evaluators.

Overview of Qualitative Research and Program Evaluation

Qualitative research is a form of exploratory inquiry that is concerned with understandings related to perceptions, reasons, and meanings. This means qualitative inquirers engage in a "meaning-making process," attempting to interpret phenomena based on the meanings people assign to them (Patton, 2015, p. 3). To make sense of phenomena, investigators gather information and materials using qualitative methods such as focus groups, individual interviews, observations, and documents. Each qualitative method uniquely contributes to the meaning-making process, rendering the phenomenon under investigation visible in a distinct way (Denzin & Lincoln, 2018).

Qualitative research as we know it today has deep sociological and anthropological roots. In his chapter on the history of qualitative research, Fredrick Erickson (2018) states antecedents to qualitative research are evident in the descriptive writings of the 5th century BCE and 2nd century

CE Greek scholars. These descriptive accounts discussed everyday social practices (traveling, fishing, dancing), which served to examine cultural differences. In addition to cross-cultural analyses, narratives were used to explore the experiences of the lower classes and people subjected to colonial rule. Erickson (2018) further explains, by the 19th century, scholars were focused on systemizing how these social practices were examined. While disagreements about how society would be studied persisted, a model of studying cultural and social practices emulating the physical sciences prevailed. This form of inquiry focused on the generalization of knowledge in its early history is what we know today as *sociology*. Anthropological scholars in the latter part of the 19th century also aimed to produce generalizable knowledge; their version of social inquiry, prioritizing cultural practices, cultural advancements, and the colonial experiences of people around the world is what we know today as *anthropology* (Erickson, 2018).

Sociologists and anthropologists from the West traveled to colonized countries to gather knowledge about and report on the cultures of different communities. However, the privileging of generalizable knowledge in both sociology and anthropology positioned the cultures studied as the objectified and exotic Others. As a result, Denzin, Lincoln, and Smith (2008) note how qualitative research, including its methods, "serves as a metaphor of colonial knowledge production, for power, and for truth." They describe the metaphor in this way:

> Research, quantitative and qualitative is scientific. Research provides the foundation for reports about and representations of the other. In the colonial context, research becomes an objective way of representing the dark-skinned other to the White world (p. 4).

The key point here is that the use of qualitative research as a colonial tool linked it to a "racist project" (Denzin and Lincoln, 2018, p. 9).

As qualitative inquiry developed, investigators became increasingly dissatisfied with the privileging of generalizable knowledge and Eurocentric frameworks and methods, which examine minority communities with a deficit model. In response, investigators relied upon critical approaches such as critical race theory and decolonizing traditions. While each critical approach and decolonizing tradition is importantly distinct, these approaches share the goal of critiquing traditional, Western, and deficit-based approaches to inquiry. Beyond critique, qualitative inquirers found these non-traditional approaches attractive as they offer alternative ways to theorize, conduct, represent and report work with minority communities. In contrast to more Eurocentric frameworks, these traditions valued minority perspectives, transformative inquiry, and participatory practices.

Over time, qualitative research expanded to other fields. For example, in the 1980s, health researchers were leading in the use of focus groups in the fields of health education and promotion (Wilkinson, 1998). The increased acceptance of qualitative methods could be seen in the fields of education, business, medicine, nursing, social work (Denzin, Lincoln, & Smith, 2008), and program evaluation (Buttram, 1990) in the 1980s as well.

Program evaluation is a form of inquiry that collects information to make judgments about a program's effectiveness or to provide feedback important for program improvement efforts. Patton, for example, suggests that evaluation, as a *practice*, dates to Biblical times (Patton, 2015). The genesis of evaluation as a *profession*, however, is formally recognized at the beginning in the 1960s and 1970s (Mertens, 2018) as these decades reflect key advancements in the field of evaluation. For instance, the field of evaluation expanded rapidly in the United States due to increased mandates to evaluate programs funded by the federal government, most notably programs with roots in the Great Society initiative, the Economic Opportunity Act, and the Manpower Development and Training Act (Alkin & King, 2016). Program evaluation, in large part, served as a mechanism to hold programs accountable for the federal funding they received. The role of program evaluators, then, was to provide evaluative data to help decision-makers determine the future of a program.

Since the 1970s, evaluation continued to expand because of enhancements in evaluation methods (Coffman, 2003/2004), the professionalization of the profession via conferences, textbooks, organizations (Patton, 1990), and greater clarification of the evaluator's role (Coffman, 2003/2004). As part of its professional evolution, evaluation developed in Europe in the 1970s, which was fueled by the need to assess the effect of the European Structural Fund and Cohesion Funds, beginning in 2004 (Mertens, 2018). In recent decades, evaluation gained more of an international presence as the need for evaluation work from international government agencies has grown (Mertens, 2018).

Like the history of qualitative research, early evaluation work privileged quantitative approaches. Later, qualitative methods became valued by evaluators. For instance, by the 1980s, program evaluators used focus groups to gather perspectives from a variety of *stakeholders* or those persons impacted by, and or who have interests in, a program. Like market researchers, program evaluators used the data from the focus groups to assess people's needs, interests, and concerns, as well as to design survey instruments (Buttram, 1990; Mitra, 1994). In addition, evaluation designs incorporated focus group methods during different phases of a program (beginning, middle, end) (Buttram, 1990), which was beneficial to assess how stakeholder needs were addressed by the program, provide data for program improvement and decision-making, as well as to make midcourse corrections. Recently, in the United States, evaluations that aim to address social, economic and political inequalities have developed. Evaluations focused on these aims are referred to as social justice-oriented evaluation approaches (Mertens & Wilson, 2012).

A prominent social justice evaluation approach, *culturally responsive evaluation*, recognizes the importance of culture and how evaluation can be more responsive to stakeholders (Hood, Hopson, & Frierson, 2015). This strand of evaluation has significantly informed what it means to be culturally responsive in the context of evaluation. Other fields such as psychology have also contributed to defining culturally responsive or culturally-anchored inquiry (Hughes, Seidman & Williams, 1993).

As a program evaluator and qualitative inquirer that works within the field of education, notions of cultural responsiveness from the field of education and program evaluation guide my work. As such, in the following section, I briefly discuss the conceptual strands related to cultural responsiveness from the fields of education and program evaluation. To conclude the chapter, I merge selected strands and explicate the stance of cultural responsiveness that I use to guide this book.

Conceptual Strands Related to Cultural Responsiveness

A strand of cultural responsiveness in the field of education was developed in response to the racial desegregation initiatives in the 1960s and 1970s.

As students from diverse backgrounds were attempting to integrate schools across the United States, some educators and researchers were seeking approaches to teach students from different cultural backgrounds appropriately (Aronson & Laughter, 2016). Two approaches in the K-12 educational literature stand out as making major contributions to teaching and learning, and also recognizing the importance of cultural differences (Aronson & Laughter, 2016). The first, *culturally responsive pedagogy*, as presented by Gloria Ladson-Billings (1994), "is designed to problematize teaching and encourage teachers to ask about the nature of the student-teacher relationship, the curriculum, schooling, and society" (Ladson-Billing, 1994, p. 483). The second, *culturally relevant education*, as discussed in the work of Geneva Gay (2002) is defined as "using the cultural characteristics, experiences, and perspectives of ethnically diverse students as conduits for teaching them more effectively" (p. 106). Whereas the main goal of culturally responsive pedagogy is to critically examine and question the nature of schooling itself, and the key objective of culturally relevant education is the development of culturally responsive learning strategies, both approaches conceptualize cultural responsiveness as centering student-culture, advancing educational equity, and viewing "the classroom as a site for social justice" (Aronson & Laughter, 2016, p. 163).

Another strand of cultural responsiveness comes from the field of educational evaluation. The literature on educational evaluation identifies early uses of culturally responsive methods by African American evaluators during the 1930s, 1940s, and 1950s in response to educational inequities, particularly in southern states (Hood, 2001; Hopson & Hood, 2005). As part of their evaluation design, these evaluators incorporated qualitative research methods to complement their quantitative methodologies. Both qualitative and quantitative approaches were considered valuable to evaluate educational inequities in segregated schools and universities. Qualitative methods, in particular, were viewed as necessary to provide a historical analysis of the schools, investigate students' perceptions of schools, and understand students' cultural backgrounds. Given the severity of racial injustice faced by African Americans, Hood (2001) asserts,

> it would have been socially irresponsible for African Americans trained in evaluation techniques to engage in evaluative efforts that

did not address the unequal educational opportunities and resources that were implicit in many northern states and explicit in the
southern ones (p. 39).

Hood's perspective on the social responsibility of these early African American evaluators is reflected in his definition of responsive evaluation. Hood
(2001) argues that "to be responsive fundamentally means to attend sub-
stantively and politically to issues of culture and race in evaluation practice"
(p. 32). The form of responsive evaluation exhibited by African American
evaluators responding to those in their community experiencing racial injustices was antecedent to Robert E. Stake's (1975) *responsive evaluation*
approach.

Stake—a prominent leader in the field of evaluation, particularly educational evaluation—advanced a responsive approach to evaluation primarily driven by stakeholders' concerns (Abma, 2005). For Stake, responsive
evaluation requires "coming to know the circumstances and problems and
values well, then using professional talent and discipline to carry out the
inquiry" (Abma & Stake, 2001, p. 9). In Stake's version of responsive evaluation, the role of a responsive evaluator is that of a "knowledge facilitator" (Abma & Stake, 2001). In this role, the responsive evaluator facilitates
learning from and between program participants, then uses the knowledge
generated to make evaluative judgments about the quality of the program.

Recently, evaluation scholars have increasingly acknowledged the role
of culture in evaluation theory and practice (Chouinard & Cousins, 2007;
Hood, Hopson, & Frierson, 2005; Hood, Hopson, & Frierson, 2015;
Kirkhart, 2010; Samuels & Ryan, 2011; Thomas & Parsons, 2017). Evaluation scholars further recognize that cultural understandings and identities
are dynamic and simultaneously occurring at both the individual and group
levels (Kirkhart, 2010). Kirkhart (2010) clarifies the intersectional dimensions of culture when she states, *culture* "represents an intersection of identifications held by individuals plus identifications of collective groupings
such as organizations, institutions, communities, societies, and nations" (p.
401). Culturally responsive evaluators utilize theories and methods that address the culture and context of program participants and critically examine
how their evaluation practice, and the field of evaluation advances (or im-

pedes) social justice and equity (Hood, Hopson, & Frierson, 2005; Hood, Hopson, & Frierson, 2015). The American Evaluation Association's (AEA) *Public Statement on Cultural Competence in Evaluation* (AEA, 2011) and *Evaluator Competencies* (AEA, 2018), for example, affirm the importance of culture in evaluation practice and provide guidance to conduct responsive evaluations. In short, *culturally responsive evaluation*:

• Welcomes diverse perspectives of program stakeholders—especially those who have been traditionally underrepresented in evaluations, and the context (Frierson, Hood, & Hughes, 2002)

• Adopts an anti-deficit-based approach to evaluation that views cultural diversity as a strength and vital resource to inform the evaluation (Thomas & Parson, 2017; Yarbrough, Shulha, Hopson, & Caruthers, 2011)

• Advances culturally sensitive evaluation theories (alternative, non-Western or Indigenous) that have been (and continue to be) marginalized in evaluation practice (Bowman, Francis, & Tyndall, 2015)

• Considers active engagement with the cultural contexts of a program imperative to determine its merit or worth (Askew, Beverly, & Jay, 2012)

Culturally responsive evaluation demands attention to culture and context through all phases of the evaluation design (Bledsoe & Donaldson, 2015). Some of the strategies utilized to conduct a culturally responsive evaluation include (Hood, Hopson, & Frierson, 2015; Thomas & Parsons, 2017):

• Using an examination of the cultural context to set boundaries for the evaluation

• Working with a diverse research team, including those that share the participants' lived experience

• Identifying stakeholders who are often overlooked or marginalized

• Developing evaluation questions that reflect a range of stakeholder issues and interests

- Using varied data sources that address evaluation questions and center stakeholders' experiences

- Considering the cultural context when analyzing, interpreting, and disseminating the data

Contemporary Focus Group Use

Contemporary social science researchers and evaluators have increasingly utilized frameworks and arranged focus groups in ways that aim to respectfully attend to the cultures and contexts of marginalized communities. For instance, guided by the Consolidated Framework for Implementation Research (Northridge et al., 2017), health researchers conducted focus groups with Dominican, African American, and Puerto Rican adults aged 50 years and older. Employing the assistance of bilingual field recruiters and conducting focus groups in Spanish were strategies used to tailor focus groups to meet the linguistic needs of the older adults prioritized for their study. Other social science researchers and evaluators—whether implicitly or explicitly—have also enlisted culturally congruent focus group strategies for marginalized groups: deaf and hard of hearing participants (Balch & Mertens, 1999), the Bangladeshi community (Fallon & Brown, 2002), Latina women (Madriz, 2003), incarcerated women (Pollock, 2003), Indigenous communities (Lavallée, 2009), lesbian, gay, bisexual, and transgender (LGBT) patients and health care providers (Wilkerson, Rybicki, Barber, & Smolenski, 2011), Black women of low socioeconomic status (Gross, Davis, Anderson, Hall, & Hilyard, 2016), African American and Caribbean-born men (Cobran, Hall, & Aiken, 2017), and children (Bokhorst-Heng & Marshall, 2019).

Recently, Rodriguez, Schwartz, Lahman, and Geist (2011) merged select qualitative research paradigms and the culturally responsive education literature to advance a notion of culturally responsive focus groups. Specifically, Rodriguez et al., (2011) rely on constructivism, feminism, Chicana feminist epistemology, critical race theory and culturally relevant teaching strategies (Farmer, Hauk & Neumann, 2005; Gay, 2002; Villegas & Lucas, 2002) to describe six characteristics of a culturally responsive inquirer. First, a culturally responsive inquirer is socially conscious, being aware of the interrelated historical, sociopolitical and socioeconomic contexts within which participants' lives are embedded, and the consequences of those contexts for participants' lives. Second, a culturally responsive inquirer promotes a strengths-based model, viewing participants' cultures as an asset rather than a deficit. Third, a culturally responsive inquirer identifies herself as an agent for change with the ability to create spaces for meaningful exchanges between participants. Fourth, a culturally responsive inquirer acknowledges how participants wish to be identified in the inquiry process. Fifth, a culturally responsive inquirer employs reflexive practices to assess how the inquirer and her inquiry practices impact the inquiry process. And sixth, a culturally responsive inquirer views the inquiry process itself as a site of knowledge expansion and co-construction.

Bringing it All Together: My Stance on Culturally Responsive Focus Groups

Thus far, I have provided a definition of focus groups, a brief history of focus groups, an overview of qualitative research and program evaluation, some background on the concept of cultural responsiveness, and a perspective on culturally responsive focus groups. Reviewing these topics was important to trace the development of focus groups and notions of cultural responsiveness. In particular, the discussion above suggests that focus groups, as a qualitative research method, are linked with the general colonial history of qualitative research as an objective and racist enterprise. Further, the discussion highlights how different fields have increasingly applied focus groups. What we learn, then, from the history of qualitative research and the application of focus groups across different fields is that focus groups are not value neutral. That is, focus groups take on the perspectives, values, methodological traditions, and goals of the inquirer. All of these in turn have implications for participants—particularly those who have been historically marginalized. Seen in this light, it is evident that notions of cultural responsiveness and tailoring focus groups to be sensitive to underrepresented, misrepresented or ignored communities matters.

My notion of cultural responsiveness is informed by the history of qualitative research, shaped by the origins of focus groups, and inspired by contemporary notions of culturally responsive focus groups. Further, my conceptualization of cultural responsiveness attempts to address the historical tensions of traditional focus groups by employing culturally congruent perspectives and strategies. So, what, then, is the notion of cultural responsiveness, and by extension culturally responsive focus group practice, that I use to guide this book? I address this question by listing the characteristics of a *culturally responsive inquirer* (see Table 1.1 *The Culturally Responsive Inquirer*).

Table 1.1: *The Culturally Responsive Inquirer*

Views cultural responsiveness as a stance that aims to advance social justice by centering participants' culture and the context within which they are embedded during the inquiry process (AEA, 2011; AEA, 2018; Gay, 2002; Ladson-Billing, 1994)
Positions herself as a lifelong learner, learning and unlearning how to value the culture of participants in the inquiry process (AEA, 2011; AEA, 2018)
Engages reflexivity, proactively questioning her own assumptions and actions throughout the inquiry process (Lahman, Geitst, Rodriguez, Graglia & DeRoche, 2011; Symonette, 2004)
Recognizes herself as interconnected with others and committed to a rational, empathic, and respectful care for participants (Lahman et al., 2011; Symonette, 2004)
Advances a strength-based approach, identifying participants' culture as an asset rather than a deficit (Yarbrough, Shulha, Hopson & Caruthers, 2011)
Perceives herself as a change-agent responsible for engaging the power and privilege inherent in social relations and creating spaces for meaningful interactions and story sharing (Rodriguez, Schwartz, Lahman, & Geist, 2011)
Provides opportunities for participants to describe who they are and how they want to be identified (Harding, 1991)
Works with participants to co-construct knowledge within the inquiry setting (Lahman et al., 2011; Rodriguez et al., 2011)
Considers culture and context important in collection, analysis, interpretation, and dissemination of data (Hood, Hopson & Frierson, 2015; Thomas & Parsons, 2017)
Operates with a sociocultural consciousness, aware of the dynamic character of culture and how individual identities (i.e., race/ethnicity, social class, age, gender) intersect with collective identities (organization, community, nation) (Hall, 2019; Kirkhart, 2010; Lahman et al., 2011)
Employs theories and methodological techniques—including non-traditional, non-Western, Indigenous approaches—that are responsive to participants' cultural contexts (AEA, 2011; 2018; Lavallée, 2009)

In general, my stance on cultural responsiveness is like other notions of cultural responsiveness in that it affirms the cultural context of participants and seeks social justice. Notwithstanding, I consider my stance on culturally responsive focus groups distinct, as it explicitly recognizes the focus group a site for social justice. As mentioned earlier, I view focus groups as a qualitative research method designed to accommodate a specific group, generate a collective conversation, and examine group culture. Based on this, I consider focus groups uniquely positioned to center the lived experiences of participants in the inquiry process. When marginalized groups are centered, I believe opportunities exist to interrogate taken-for-granted assumptions, challenge stereotypes, include voices that are often excluded or stifled, and disrupt oppressive practices, thereby advancing social justice.

Summary

In sum, the culturally responsive focus group practice I present in this book envisions and explores the myriad ways culturally responsive focus groups can be understood and implemented. Ultimately, I hope to inspire you to imagine how focus groups can be responsively designed for the particular community you plan to engage.

References

Abma, T. A. (2005). Responsive evaluation: Its meaning and special contribution to health promotion. *Evaluation and Program Planning, 28*(3), 279–289.

Abma, T. A., & Stake, R. E. (2001). Responsive evaluation, roots and evolution. *New Directions for Evaluation, 92,* 7–22.

Alkin, M., & King, J. (2016). The historical development of evaluation use. *American Journal of Evaluation, 37*(4), 568–579.

American Evaluation Association. (2011). *Statement on cultural competence in evaluation.* Retrieved from www. eval.org/ccstatment.asp

American Evaluation Association. (2018). *Evaluator competencies.* Retrieved from www.eval.org/page/competencies

Aronson, B., & Laughter, J. (2016). The theory and practice of culturally relevant education: A synthesis of research across content areas. *Review of Educational Research, 86*(1) 163–206.

Askew, K., Beverly, M. G., & Jay, M. L. (2012). Aligning collaborative and culturally responsive evaluation approaches. *Evaluation and Program Planning, 35*(4), 552–557.

Balch, G. I., & Mertens, D. M. (1999). Focus group design and group dynamics: Lessons from deaf and hard of hearing participants. *American Journal of Evaluation, 20,* 265–277.

Beldsoe, K., & Donaldson, S. I. (2015). Culturally responsive theory-driven evaluations. In S. Hood, R. Hopsons, K. Obeidat, & H. Frierson (Eds.). *Continuing the journey to reposition culture and cultural context in evaluation theory and practice.* Greenwich, NY: Information Age.

Bokhorst-Heng, W., & Keating Marshall, K. (2019) Informing research (practices) through pedagogical theory: Focus groups with adolescents. *International Journal of Research & Method in Education, 42*(2), 148–162.

Bowman, N. R., Dodge Francis, C., Tyndall, M. (2015). Culturally responsive Indigenous evaluation: A practical approach for evaluating Indigenous projects in tribal reservation contexts. In S. Hood, R. Hopson, & H. Frierson. (Eds.), *Continuing the Journey to Reposition Culture and Cultural Context in Evaluation Theory and Practice* (pp. 335–360). Charlotte, NC: Information Age Publishing.

Buttram, J. L. (1990). Focus groups: A starting point for needs assessment. *American Journal of Evaluation, 11,* 207–212.

Chouinard, J., & Cousins, B. (2007). Culturally competent valuation for aboriginal communities: A review of the empirical literature. *Journal of Multidisciplinary Evaluation, 4,* 40–57.

Cobran, E., Hall, J. N., & Aiken, W. (2018). African-American and Caribbean-born men's perceptions of prostate cancer fear and facilitators for screening behavior: A pilot study. *Journal of Cancer Education, 33*(3), 640–648.

Coffman, J. (2003/2004). Ask the expert: Michael Scriven on the differences between evaluation and social science research. *The Evaluation Exchange, 9*(4).

Cox, K., Higginbotham, J., & Burton, J. (1976). Applications of focus group interviews in marketing. *Journal of Marketing, 40*(1), 77.

Denzin, N. & Lincoln, Y. (2018). *The Sage Handbook of Qualitative Research.* Thousand Oaks, LA: Sage.

Denzin, N., Lincoln, Y., & Smith, L. (Eds.). (2008). *Handbook of critical and Indigenous methodologies,* Los Angeles, CA: Sage.

Erickson, F. (2011). A history of qualitative inquiry in social and educational research. In N. Denzin & Y. Lincoln (Eds.). *The SAGE handbook of qualitative research* (4th ed., pp. 43–59). Thousand Oaks, CA: Sage.

Fallon, G., & Brown, R. B. (2002). Focusing on focus groups: Lessons from a research project involving a Bangladeshi community. *Qualitative Research, 2*(2), 195–208.

Farmer, J., Hauk, S., & Neumann, A. M. (2005). Negotiating reform: Implementing process standards in culturally responsive professional development. *The High School Journal, 88*(4), 59–71.

Frierson, H. T., Hood, S., & Hughes, G. B. (2002). Strategies that address culturally responsive evaluation. In J. Frechtling (Ed.), *The 2002 user-friendly handbook for project evaluation* (pp. 63–73). Arlington, VA: National Science Foundation.

Gay, G. (2002). Preparing for culturally responsive teaching. *Journal of Teacher Education, 53,* 106–116.

Gross, T., Davis, M., Anderson, A., Hall, J., Hilyard, K. (2016). Long-term breast-feeding in African-American mothers: A positive deviance inquiry of WIC participants. *Journal of Human Lactation, 33*(1), 128–139.

Harding, S. (1991). *Whose science? Whose knowledge? Thinking from women's lives.* Ithaca, NY: Cornell University Press.

Hood, S. (2001). Nobody knows my name: in praise of African American evaluators who were responsive. *New Directions for Evaluation, 92*, 31–43.

Hood, S., Hopson, R., & Frierson, H. (Eds.). (2015). *Continuing the journey to reposition culture and cultural context in evaluation theory and practice.* Greenwich, CT: Information Age.

Hopson, R., & Hood, S. (2005). An untold story in evaluation roots: Reid Jackson and his contributions toward culturally responsive evaluation at Three-Fourths Century. In S. Hood, R. K. Hopson, and H. T. Frierson (Eds.). *The role of culture and cultural context: A mandate for inclusion, the discovery of truth, and understanding in evaluative theory and practice.* Greenwich, CT: Information Age Publishing, Inc.

Hughes, D., Seidman, E., & Williams, N. (1993). Cultural phenomena and the research enterprise: Toward a culturally anchored methodology. *American Journal of Community Psychology, 21*, 687–703.

Kidd, P., & Parshall, M. (2000). Getting the focus and the group: enhancing analytical rigor in focus group research. *Qualitative Health Research, 10*(30), 293–308.

Kirkhart, K. E. (2010). Eyes on the prize: Multicultural validity and evaluation theory. *American Journal of Evaluation, 31*, 400–413.

Krueger, R. & Casey, M. (2015). *Focus groups: A practical guide for applied research* (5th ed.). Thousand Oaks, CA: Sage Publications, Inc.

Ladson-Billings, G. (1994). *The dreamkeepers.* San Francisco, CA: Jossey-Bass.

Lavellée, L. (2009). Practical application of an Indigenous research framework and two qualitative Indigenous research methods: Sharing circles and Anishnaabe symbol-based reflection. *International Journal of Qualitative Methods, 8*(1), 21–40.

Madriz, E. (2003). Focus groups in feminist research. In N. K. Denzin, & Y. S. Lincoln (Eds.), *Collecting and interpreting qualitative materials* (pp. 363–388). Thousand Oaks, CA: Sage.

Massey, O. T. (2011). A proposed model for the analysis and interpretation of focus groups in evaluation research. *Evaluation and Program Planning, 34*, 21–28.

Mertens, D. (2018). *Mixed methods design in evaluation.* Thousand Oaks, CA: Sage.

Mertens, D., & Wilson, A. (2012). *Program evaluation theory and practice* (2nd ed.). Thousand Oaks, CA: Sage.

Merton, R. K., & Kendall, P. (1946). The focused interview. *American Journal of Sociology, 51*, 541–557.

Merton, R. K., Fiske, M., & Kendall, P. L. (1990). *The focused interview* (2nd ed.). New York, NY: The Free Press.

Mitra, A. (1994). Use of focus groups in the design of recreation needs assessment questionnaires. *Evaluation and Program Planning, 17*, 133–140.

Morgan, D. (2019). *Basic and advanced focus groups.* Thousand Oaks, LA: Sage.

Northridge, M., Shedlin, M., Schrimshaw, E., Estrada, I., Da La Cruz, L., Peralta, R., Bridsall, S., Metcaff, S., Chakrabort, B., & Kunzel, C. (2017). Recruitment of racial/ethnic minority older adults through community sites for focus group discussions. *BMC Public Health, 17*(1).

Patton, M.Q. (1990). The challenge of being a profession. *Evaluation Practice, 11*(1), 45–51.

Patton, M.Q. (2015). *Qualitative research and evaluation methods* (4th ed.). Sage Publications, Thousand Oaks.

Pollack, S. (2003). Focus-group methodology in research with incarcerated women: Race, power, and collective experience. *Affilia, 18*, 461–472.

Rodriguez, K., Schwartz, J., Lahman, M., & Geist, M. (2011). Culturally responsive focus groups: Reframing the research experience to focus on participants. *The International Journal of Qualitative Methods, 10*(4), 400–417.

Ryan, K., Ganda, T., Culbertson, M., & Carlson, C. (2013). Focus groups evidence: Implications for design and analysis. *American Journal of Evaluation, 35*(3), 328–345.

Samuels, M., & Ryan, K. (2011). Grounding evaluations in culture. *American Journal of Evaluation, 32*(2), 183–198.

Stake, R. E. (1975). To evaluate an arts program. In R. E. Stake (Ed.), *Evaluating the arts in education: A responsive approach* (pp. 13-31). Columbus, OH: Merrill.

Symonette, H. (2004). Walking pathways toward becoming culturally competent evaluator: Boundaries, borderlanes, and border crossings. In M. Thompson-Robinson, R. Hopson, & S. SenGupta (Eds.), In *search of cultural competence in evaluation: Toward principles and practices. New Directions for Evaluation, 102*, 95–109.

Thomas, V., & Parsons, B. (2017). Culturally responsive evaluation meets systems-oriented evaluation, *American Journal of Evaluation, 38*(1), 7–28.

Villegas, A. & Lucas, T. (2002). Preparing culturally responsive teachers: Rethinking the curriculum. *Journal of Teacher Education, 53*(1), 20–32.

Wilkerson, J. M., Rybicki, S., Barber, C. A., & Smolenski, D. J. (2011). Creating a culturally competent clinical environment for LGBT patients. *Journal of Gay & Lesbian Social Services, 23*(3), 376–394.

Wilkinson, S. (1998). Focus group methodology: A review. *International Journal of Social Research Methodology: Theory & Practice, 1*, 181–203.

Yarbrough, D. B., Shulha, L. M., Hopson, R. K., & Caruthers, F. A. (2011). *The program evaluation standards: A guide for evaluators and evaluation users* (3rd ed.). Thousand Oaks, CA: Sage.

CHAPTER TWO

Design

In This Chapter

- Interactive Design

  – Goals, Theories, and Questions

- Design Options

- Appropriateness of Focus Groups

- Sampling

- Recruitment

- Number of Focus Group Participants

- Ethics

- Summary

I BEGIN THIS CHAPTER drawing from Maxwell's (2013) *interactive design* scholarship. His notion of interactive design suggests that all components (goals, theories, questions, etc.) interact and influence each other, which is especially the case for studies that involve qualitative methods, including focus groups. I view Maxwell's perspective on interactive design useful for theorizing or thinking about how you and elements of your design can be responsive not only to the goals of the inquiry project but also to participants' lived experiences. Building on Maxwell's conceptualization of interactive design, I then discuss specific design components and offer some design options. Next, I review the appropriateness of focus groups for your design, common focus group sampling techniques, and strategies for recruiting focus group participants. The chapter concludes with recommendations for the number of participants to include in a focus group as well as a discussion on ethical issues pertinent to focus groups.

Interactive Design

In qualitative research, a design reflects a plan for how the inquiry will be conducted, including various inquiry components (theories, questions, etc.) and procedures for how the components will be carried out. Traditional notions of design conceptualize the plan as procedures occurring in sequential order. However, Maxwell's (2013) notion of an interactive design reframes this traditional notion of design. Inquiry itself is not a linear process with procedures occurring one after the other in sequential order. Therefore, according to Maxwell (2013), a design cannot be conceptualized (or presented) as a linear process. This is because the design components continuously respond to each other; they interact in ways that cannot always be predicted in advance (Maxwell, 2013). Furthermore, the notion of interactive design suggests that designs require reflexivity on the part of the researcher. This means, as an inquirer, you will need to continually assess how your design is actually working during the research and how it influences and is influenced by the context in which you're operating, and to make adjustments and changes so that your study can accomplish what you want (Maxwell, 2013, p. 3).

It is from this perspective, Maxwell (2013) contends, that a design is a "real entity" with "real consequences" (p. 3). Here we note how Maxwell's notion of interactive design acknowledges and is attentive to the consequential nature of inquiry and the impact it has on people's lives.

In sum, the notion of interactive design suggests that inquiry design should be understood as an interactive enterprise where the inquirer is responsible for reflexively constructing and reconstructing the design based on (1) how the design components are working in relation to each other, (2) the extent to which the design is responsive to the context, and (3) the potential consequences of the design components for participants (Maxwell, 2013).

In the following sections, building on Maxwell's notion of interactive design, I review design components and how they are intended to interact or inform each other.

Goals

Cultural responsiveness includes an examination of one's goals and purposes for conducting inquiry. In alignment with this perspective, Maxwell (2013) argues for assessments of inquiry goals and considers such examinations a key component of inquiry design.

Maxwell (2013) offers three kinds of inquiry goals to critically examine when designing your study: personal, practical, and intellectual. Personal goals are goals that motivate you but not necessarily anyone else. Your personal goals are informed by your values, experiences, attitudes, biases, and assumptions. Failure to deal with your personal goals can contribute to biased findings and negative outcomes for participants (House, 2017; Kirkhart, 2015). Intellectual goals are based on general inquiry purposes such as conducting an inquiry to investigate the past, or increase understanding. While intellectual goals provide an overall frame for the inquiry, practical goals "are focused on *accomplishing* [emphasis in original] something—meeting some need, changing some situation, or achieving some objective" (Maxwell, 2013, p. 28). Practical goals address the social justice aims of culturally responsive focus groups in that these goals are focused on the needs and concerns of others. An important question to ask here would be how will the design and its components serve to affirm and empower focus group participants.

Overall, scrutinizing your inquiry purposes is valuable to clarify (1) your motivations for conducting the study, (2) areas of interest and issues related to your topic, (3) the rationale for your design (Maxwell, 2013), and (4) how social justice will be addressed.

Theories

The word theory has been defined in varied ways. Yet, a common point made across different definitions suggests that a theory is "a particular kind of explanation" (Tavallaei & Talib, 2010). Because a wide range of theories exists, it is critical to understand the roles different types of theory play in in-

quiry design. Here, I briefly review two types of theories qualitative researchers use to inform their designs: conceptual frameworks and paradigms.

Conceptual frameworks. To better understand the complexity of a topic
or phenomenon of interest, researchers examine the related literature. Other
sources of information such as discussions with practitioners and scholars
from various disciplines are also relied upon to gain in-depth understandings
of a phenomenon (Jabareen, 2009; Maxwell, 2013). Collecting information
allows the inquirer to identify key concepts and central ideas. Regardless of
disciplinary origin, the identified network of concepts helps to frame what
is currently understood about the phenomenon (Jabareen, 2009). This framing, or conceptual framework, is considered a *"tentative theory* [emphasis
in original]" (Maxwell, 2013, p. 39) as the network of concepts explains
the process of and defines what constitutes the phenomenon. Conceptual
frameworks are an essential design component, informing inquiry goals,
inquiry questions, and use of focus groups in the design (Maxwell, 2013).

Qualitative researchers from different disciplinary backgrounds apply
conceptual frameworks to their design to investigate a phenomenon of interest. For example, I reviewed relevant literature to understand what a school
needs to implement an effective reform initiative—the topic of my study.
Based on my review of the literature (Newmann, King, & Rigdon, 1997),
I identified concepts that became the *collective capacity* conceptual framework (Hall, 2010). As a theory, collective capacity suggests schools have
powerful potential to implement reform initiatives effectively if they can
collectively organize leadership, instruction, decision making, and resources
toward shared teaching and learning goals. Figure 2.1, *Collective Capacity Conceptual Framework* shows how interrelated dimensions constitute
collective capacity and how the dimensions are intended to work together.
I applied the collective capacity conceptual framework in the development
and design of my own case study (Hall, 2010).

Paradigms. Another kind of theory used to inform qualitative inquiry
designs is called a paradigm. Paradigms are more abstract, in contrast to
a conceptual framework; this is because a paradigm reflects philosophical
assumptions or broad explanations about how the world works. Paradigms
have been defined many ways (Greene & Hall, 2010; Kuhn, 1996; Morgan,
2007). One definition of a paradigm suggests it includes core assumptions
or beliefs regarding axiology, epistemology, and ontology (Denzin & Lin-

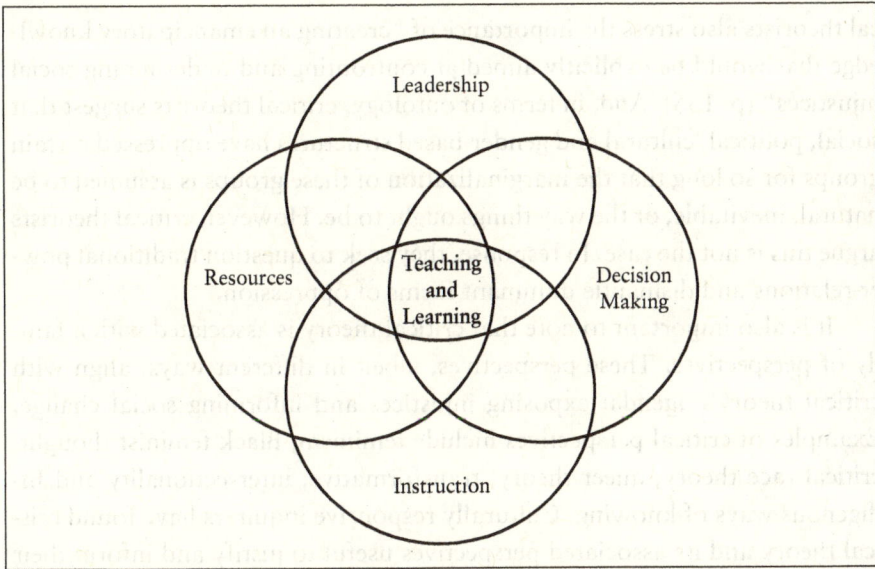

Figure 2.1: *Collective Capacity Conceptual Framework*[1]

coln, 2018; Schwandt, 1989). According to Denzin and Lincoln (2018), axiology is about ethics and values. Epistemology concerns how one comes to know the world or what constitutes knowledge. And, ontology relates to the nature of reality.

The paradigm most closely associated with the culturally responsive stance advanced in this book is critical theory. Critical theory is associated with scholars of the Frankfurt School (i.e., Max Horkheimer, Theodore Adorno). The work of these scholars was influenced by, and in response to, Marxian philosophy. Briefly, in terms of axiology, critical theorists value "social critique and praxis" as they are considered imperative to bring about social change (Prasad, 2018, p. 167). This means critical theorists value inquiry that connects theory to action in order to disrupt the status quo and advance social justice. Epistemologically, critical theorists assume that knowledge is "mediated by power relations that are socially and historically constituted" (Kincheloe & McLaren, 1994 [as cited in Prasad, 2018]). Criti-

1 Adapted from "Investigating international accountability and collective capacity: Taking a closer look at mathematics instruction" by J. N. Hall, 2010, *Journal of Curriculum and Instruction*, 4(2), 9–32.

cal theorists also stress the importance of "creating an emancipatory knowledge that would be explicitly aimed at confronting and undermining social injustices" (p. 155). And, in terms of ontology, critical theorists suggest that social, political, cultural and gender-based structures have oppressed certain groups for so long that the marginalization of these groups is assumed to be natural, inevitable, or the way things ought to be. However, critical theorists argue this is not the case. In response, they seek to question traditional power relations and dismantle dominant forms of oppression.

It is also important to note that critical theory is associated with a family of perspectives. These perspectives, albeit in different ways, align with critical theory's agenda: exposing injustices and informing social change. Examples of critical perspectives include feminism, Black feminist thought, critical race theory, queer theory, transformative, intersectionality and Indigenous ways of knowing. Culturally responsive inquirers have found critical theory and its associated perspectives useful to justify and inform their designs. That is, they use theories and or allied perspectives as tools to support how their design and the components therein can engage marginalized communities and potentially mobilize action. Some of these perspectives (Black feminist thought, intersectionality, Indigenous ways of knowing) and how they inform a specific focus group approach are described in more detail later in the book (see Chapter 5). For now, an important point to understand is that theories (conceptual frameworks, paradigms, and their related perspectives) importantly contribute to your inquiry design by highlighting central aspects of the phenomenon worthy of investigation and explicating the worldview or assumptions that undergird the investigation.

Questions

Another component of your design includes the inquiry questions. Inquiry questions are important because they are the "heart of your research design" and "will have an influence on, and should be responsive to, every other part of your study" (Maxwell, 2013, p. 73). This implies you will continuously reflect on your questions and their relationship to the other design components and make modifications accordingly. These adjustments are expected and reflect the interactive nature of qualitative research design (Maxwell, 2013). To formulate inquiry questions and investigate the relationship of the inquiry questions with other design components, Maxwell (2013) offers questions inquirers can ask themselves. A modified version of Maxwell's (2013) questions is provided below. See Maxwell (2013) for the full discussion of different ways to develop your research questions.

What are the gaps in, or tensions between, your knowledge and existing theories?

What would addressing these inquiry questions tell you that you don't already know?

How will answering these specific inquiry questions help you achieve your personal, practical, or intellectual goal/purposes?

How do these questions form a coherent set that will guide your inquiry? (Maxwell, 2013, p. 84)

Other research texts provide a more robust discussion on qualitative inquiry question development and program evaluation question formation than space here allows (Frierson, Hood, Hughes, & Thomas, 2010; Johnson & Christensen, 2014; Roulston, 2010). Such texts should be reviewed for detailed guidance. A key point of this book, and what I would like to emphasize here is that a culturally responsive stance not only considers how questions address inquiry goals but also how they attend to issues of social justice or equity as relevant to the context. For example, in a culturally responsive evaluation examining the science, technology, engineering, and mathematics (STEM) education curriculum of a public high school (Hillside High), issues of equity were focused on supporting students who are traditionally underrepresented and underserved in STEM education. Within this context, the stated evaluation purpose—in consultation with the school district—was to "assess how well the structure and content of the school's math program engaged and supported diverse students' math learning, with special focus on students who were least well served" (Hall, Ahn, & Greene, 2012, p. 203). To reflect this purpose, the evaluation questions addressed the following (Hall et al., 2012, p. 203):

- How and with what rationale are math pathways at Hillside High structured?

- In what ways does the structure support equitable opportunities to learn across the diversity of the school's student population?

Again, your questions will change as you develop your design, thinking carefully about how to attend to your purposes, theories, the needs of focus group participants and so on.

Design Options

To a large extent, your design or methodology reflects the goals (intellectual, personal, and practical) of the inquiry project. There are numerous design options available to qualitative researchers. Some of these include focus group design, ethnography, case study, narrative, phenomenology, grounded theory, and participatory action research. It is important to note that each design option has a unique way of conceptualizing the research questions, the phenomena of interest, the researcher's role, what constitutes data, how evidence is considered, and so on. Therefore, you are encouraged to further investigate the relevancy of a qualitative design for the goals and purposes of your particular project (see, for example, Denzin & Lincoln, 2018 and Patton, 2015).

Although a comprehensive review of each qualitative design type is beyond the scope of this book, in the sections that follow, some common qualitative designs are briefly described. After each description, an example illustrating how focus groups were incorporated is offered to encourage thinking about how focus groups, as part of a particular design, might be considered. While not all design option examples take an explicit culturally responsive stance, they do feature focus groups with hard-to-reach, vulnerable and marginalized groups.

Focus group design. A focus group design relies solely on focus groups to provide rich qualitative data on a topic of interest. This design is commonly used to examine an underexplored topic or discuss a sensitive issue. For instance, Singletary (2019) used a focus group design to study the effects of traumatic experiences on the psychological disposition of Black males living in violent communities. In this study, two focus groups were completed with 12 participants in total. Results suggested the importance of developing a nuanced understanding of the trauma that impacts individuals on a daily basis.

Ethnographic design. Ethnographic design involves researchers immersing themselves in an environment for an extended period to examine a culture or aspects of a culture (Van Maanen, 2011). This design has roots in anthropology and involves fieldwork (i.e., observations and interviews) lasting anywhere from several weeks to several years to understand the social relationships of a particular group of people. O'Carroll and Wainwright (2019) used an ethnographic design to examine trends in healthcare use among homeless individuals in Dublin, Ireland in three sites for five hours a week over 15 months. Ethnographic data in this study included focus groups and semi-structured interviews. Results from this study suggested a model of individuals' personal backgrounds interacting with social, economic, and structural backgrounds to create barriers to healthcare utilization in this population.

Case study design. A case study design aims to gain an in-depth understanding of a case or phenomenon of interest (Stake, 1995). Case study designs require the researcher to determine the boundaries of the case and use diverse types of data to examine the case (Yin, 2011). Munje (2019) used a case study design to explore the professional conduct of teachers in poor communities located in South Africa. In this study, the "case" being examined was teacher professionalism. To examine the case, this study included ethnographic observations, interviews, and focus groups with teachers, students, and principals. Results indicated multiple interrelated factors affecting teachers' professional conduct.

Narrative design. Narrative design aims to understand how people make meaning of their lives through the narratives, or stories, they tell (Johnson-Bailey, 2004). This design involves an in-depth analysis of small samples that typically include interviews and artifacts. Results are not always presented in chronological order, but rather, focus on the patterns identified and represented in stories. McEntee-Atalianis and Litosseliti (2017) explored the gendered narratives of persons working as speech and language therapists. Their study included six focus groups with 33 participants, in addition to other modes of data collection such as semi-structured interviews. Their analysis of the narratives or "small stories" generated from the focus group and interview data indicated how assumptions about what constitutes "women's" and "men's" work impacts the number of men and women entering the field of speech and language therapy as well as the professional choices women and men make within the field.

Phenomenological design. Phenomenological research involves an attempt to understand how a person makes sense of a lived experience (Bentz & Shapiro, 1998). This design has roots in two branches of philosophical thought: phenomenology (philosophy) and hermeneutics (Smith, Flowers, & Larkin, 2009). Phenomenology (philosophy) is concerned with the way people gain knowledge in the world, as influenced by language, thoughts, feelings, and physical experience. Hermeneutics is, broadly, textual analysis. Inquirers use phenomenology to understand the lived experience from another person's point of view and to appreciate the social and cultural context that may influence that outlook. For example, Sharp (2019) used focus groups and phenomenological analysis to examine the experience of stress in persons living with dementia. In her study, 21 individuals living with dementia participated in one of five focus groups in different regions across Scotland. Reported experiences with dementia revolved around feelings of grief, challenges involving relationships with others (family), stress managing the symptoms of dementia, and learning how to do daily activities differently.

Grounded theory design. A grounded theory design is concerned with constructing a theory that is 'grounded' in the data being studied (Charmaz, 2014). This is accomplished through a highly inductive, iterative, multistep process involving simultaneous data collection and analysis. Studies using grounded theory begin with general questions about a social topic. Researchers immerse themselves in the data through constant analysis and reflection intending to discover emergent themes. These emergent themes are continually refined until analysis approaches saturation (e.g., no new themes emerge from further data collection and analysis). Based on the analysis of themes, a theory is constructed. Dunbar, Carter, and Brown (2018) utilized focus groups as part of a grounded theory study designed to study parents' experiences and perceptions of hospice for children. In this study, six focus groups were conducted with a total of 21 parents. This study resulted in a theory that outlines the "cognitive journey" of parents and children who chose to receive hospice care.

Participatory action research design. Participatory action research (PAR) collaboratively involves researchers with stakeholders to address issues that are pertinent to their community and then take action to address those problems (Power & Allaman, 2012). Stakeholders are involved in all aspects of the study including identifying the research questions, refining the study design, data collection, interpretation of results, and the implementation/dissemination of those results. Prince, et al. (2019) used focus groups in their participatory action research study of building palliative care capacity in Canada. Those who were unable to attend focus groups completed individual interviews. In total, 62 focus groups and interviews were completed with 185 individuals across four communities. Results informed culturally appropriate resources for educating community members about palliative care.

Mixed methods design. A mixed methods design commonly includes the mixing of qualitative and quantitative methods but can also include the mixing of other design components (i.e., theories) (Greene, 2007; Greene & Hall, 2010; Hall & Greene, 2019). Components can be arranged in the order best suited for the study. Alatinga and Williams (2019) used a mixed methods design to identify very poor households who might be eligible for insurance subsidies in Ghana. In this study 24 focus groups were completed to identify patterns and characteristics of the very poor. Based on the qualitative data, a survey was developed and completed by 417 households to identify predictors of poverty. Finally, the qualitative and quantitative data were explored together to identify areas of concordance and discordance.

Appropriateness of Focus Groups

To decide if focus groups make sense for the specific design and the participants you plan to engage, a basic understanding of the method is needed. To become more familiar with the method, let's take a moment to review how focus groups are defined, identify when they are appropriate, and explore their major advantages and disadvantages.

As described in Chapter 1, focus groups are a qualitative research method designed to generate information about a specific topic through a group discussion (Krueger & Casey, 2015; Morgan, 2019; Patton, 2015; Ryan,

Ganda, Culbertson, & Carlson, 2013). Focus groups are unique in that they facilitate collective interactions, rapidly producing insights into people's experiences and opinions. Focus groups, then, are appropriate to understand group dynamics and obtain information on the needs, perceptions, and attitudes of a group. Focus group discussions are effective to deliver information about why people think the way they do and reveal areas of convergence and divergence within a group, thereby contributing rich data. Furthermore, as a result of the collective experience of being in a group discussion, participants can generate different ideas that would be unlikely to emerge within the framework of an individual interview.

Researchers have described how focus groups are particularly appropriate for inquiry with marginalized groups (Madriz, 1998; Wilkinson, 1999). This is because focus groups can potentially flatten the power hierarchy that exists between the researcher and participants. In addition, researchers note how focus groups can provide insights on how oppression is experienced and disrupt negative stereotypes related to marginalized social identities (socioeconomic status, gender, sexuality, etc.) (Halcomb, Gholizadeh, DiGiacomo, Philips, & Davidson, 2007; Madriz, 1998; Pollack, 2003; Wilkinson, 1998). Moreover, culturally responsive inquirers have found focus groups suitable when assessing various programs and interventions (Gaston, Porter & Thomas, 2007), and developing interventions for culturally and linguistically diverse populations (Halcomb et al., 2007).

Researchers note how focus groups are also beneficial to develop questionnaires. Specifically, focus group data can identify the domains that need be measured in a questionnaire, establish the dimensions that constitute each domain or what is covered in each domain, and inform wording for questionnaire items (Barrett & Kirk, 2000; Morgan, 1996; Morgan, 2019). In addition, focus group data are useful to develop other methods (i.e., questions for individual interviews, observational techniques) and clarify contradictory findings from other data sources (Merton & Kendall, 1946). Furthermore, as mentioned in Chapter 1, market researchers claim focus groups are advantageous to obtain perspectives on services and products (Cox, Higginbotham & Burton, 1976). Last, the effectiveness of focus groups in giving access to a wide range of perspectives from multiple participants during one session is another noteworthy advantage.

Despite the many advantages of focus groups, there are some disadvantages. First, focus groups may not be suitable when discussing highly controversial topics (see discussion on heterogeneous groups below). Second, there are issues concerning confidentiality when conducting focus groups. There is no guarantee that a participant will not disclose information shared during a focus group. Third, to allow participants an opportunity to share their perceptions, a limited number of questions can be asked during a focus group session. And fourth, the effectiveness of a focus group heavily relies on the skills of the moderator to facilitate the group conversation, manage group dynamics including potential conflicts, and to monitor participants' nonverbal responses and comfort level. Table 2.1 *Advantages and Disadvantages of Using Focus Groups*, summarizes the major advantages and disadvantages of focus groups.

Table 2.1: *Advantages and Disadvantages of Using Focus Groups*

Advantages
• Provides information on group dynamics and perceptions • Interactions among participants in group enhance data quality • Collective perspectives generated from a focus group can deepen understandings • Affords opportunities to shift power from researcher to participants • Group discussion can reveal how oppression is experienced by the group and serve to disrupt negative stereotypes • Rich source of data for developing other methods and informing interventions • Useful to clarify findings from other methods • Allows access to a range of perspectives and multiple people at one time
Disadvantages
• May not be suitable for highly controversial topics • Issues with confidentiality • Limited number of questions • Moderator must be highly trained in facilitating the group

Once you have decided focus groups are appropriate for your design, you will need to determine your sampling technique(s).

Sampling

Sampling in qualitative research refers to how your participants will be selected. Sampling is decidedly informed by the other design components such as relevant theories, research questions, goals and so on. Sampling in qualitative research is intended to be purposeful. That is, qualitative inquirers select participants because of the rich information they can offer related to the purposes of the investigation (Patton, 2015). Below, I review frequently used sampling techniques when selecting (and organizing) focus group participants.

Snowball sampling. Snowball sampling involves participants or others in the researcher's network recommending future participants for focus group participation (Patton, 2015). Snowball sampling is most often applied when participants are difficult to reach or locate. This approach to sampling is advantageous because the investigator receives assistance with recruitment efforts. However, there are additional things to note about snowball sampling. First, when a researcher receives assistance with the recruitment process, she also relinquishes some control over the process to recruiters. Second, the sample from this approach is limited to the recruiters' networks.

Homogenous sampling. Homogenous sampling involves selecting participants based on a predetermined set of criteria (Patton, 2015). Often, inquirers that work with marginalized communities conduct focus groups with participants that share an experience and demographic characteristics. Yet, participants do not need to have all characteristics in common, only those most relevant to the project (Krueger & Casey, 2015). For example, in a study examining African American mothers' use of online communities to sustain breastfeeding duration, participants varied in terms of geographic location, age, income level, and breastfeeding duration. However, they were all mothers who (1) identify as African American, (2) breastfed, and (3) participated in an online breastfeeding support group (e.g., Facebook) at the time of data collection (Robinson, Davis, Hall, Laukner, & Anderson, 2019).

If the focus group is homogenous, it can make it a bit easier for participants to identify similarities across participants and move the conversation forward in a generative manner. However, if participants have too much in common, it could impede the robustness of the conversation by not allowing enough diversity of opinion, because hearing about other participants' similar experiences can establish an environment of support (Morgan, 2019) and, as a result, facilitate more interactions across group participants.

Heterogeneous groups. Heterogeneous focus groups or mixed groups are less utilized among researchers due to multiple limitations. First, when participants have an exceptionally wide range of experiences, assumptions, or perceptions about a topic, it becomes challenging for participants to relate to each other (Bloor, Frankland, Thomas & Stewart, 2001; Morgan, 2019). Bloor et al., (2001) warn against heterogeneous groups when participants have perspectives that are fundamentally opposed to each other. One could imagine the potentially damaging consequences of having abortion advocates in the same focus group as pro-life advocates. In such cases, it might be more appropriate to separate these groups. Second, convening a mixed group can also result in the enactment of social norms. For example, Krueger and Casey (2015) point out, in the case with spouses, the less talkative partner defers to the more talkative partner. Being culturally responsive, then, would have you think well about the power dynamics within a focus group that can stifle less dominate focus group members (Bloor et al., 2001). Limitations notwithstanding, however, heterogeneous focus groups can be beneficial. Participants may eventually come to understand each other during the focus group discussion, presenting opportunities for valuable insights (Morgan, 2019).

Pre-existing groups. Pre-existing focus groups include participants that already have a relationship with each other. Examples of pre-existing groups might include family groups (i.e., siblings, grandmother, and granddaughter) or club members. For instance, in a study examining how schools negotiate state and district educational policies, I conducted a focus group with the sixth-grade teachers at the middle school. Because they taught the same content area, these teachers worked as a group. All the sixth-grade teachers in the middle school attended the focus groups session, evidencing Bloor et al.'s, (2001) point that pre-existing group members are more likely to "feel a sense of shared obligation to attend" the focus group session (p. 23).

Investigators may find it advantageous to conduct a focus group with a pre-existing group during an established meeting time. For example, the focus group conducted with sixth-grade teachers was held during their scheduled planning period. I also made sure to keep the duration of the group session within their established meeting time (45 minutes).

When participants have a pre-existing relationship, they can reconstruct shared memories and experiences, fill in each other's memory gaps or correct each other's memory of a particular experience (Wilkinson, 1999).

Also, pre-existing groups tend to be appropriate when discussing a potentially stigmatized experience or status (domestic violence, homelessness, HIV status), as participants can "gain reassurance when realizing that feelings, behaviors, and uncertainties are shared by others" (Bloor et al., 2001). At the same time, I should point out that while pre-existing groups have advantages, focus groups with strangers can also have advantages. Sometimes people feel more comfortable expressing feelings and emotions to focus group members they don't know (Bloor, et al., 2001). Focus groups with strangers can also lessen people's burden of worrying about how their reputation might be affected within their community.

Segmentation. Separating groups based on a category or what Morgan (2019) refers to as segmentation is another way to think about organizing participants for a focus group. To explore this topic, let's return to the investigation of how African American mothers sustain breastfeeding through online support groups on Facebook. Focus groups used for that study were initially segmented by stages of postpartum. For example, because breastfeeding duration may be impacted by a mother's experience with postpartum, two of the total four focus groups included African American mothers who experienced postpartum depression within the first six months of giving birth. African American mothers who experienced postpartum depression within the first six months were further divided into a group of mothers younger than 30 years of age and a group of mothers older than 30 years of age. Grouping mothers by a certain age provided a more comfortable setting for mothers to discuss their experiences with postpartum depression. This example reinforces Morgan's (2019) point, which is that focus group participants can be categorized or grouped in more than one way.

Successive focus groups. Successive focus groups involve focus groups with the same participants at different times. Conducting a focus group with the same people before and after an intervention, for example, has the potential to yield generative insights. However, having the same participants return for successive meetings can be challenging. This is because participants' interests and situations may change over time (Parker & Tritter, 2006). Ultimately, all sampling techniques and approaches to organizing focus groups have strengths and limitations, which, in turn, have implications for the scope of knowledge that can be generated.

To conclude this discussion, I examine other components essential to consider when designing an inquiry project. These components include recruitment strategies and the number of focus group participants. A discussion on ethical considerations emphasizing institutional review boards and consent forms rounds out the chapter.

Recruitment

Researchers and program evaluators rely on people's participation to carry out their inquiry design. Therefore, recruitment efforts matter. When seeking potential participants, especially those from hard-to-reach, underrepresented or marginalized communities, a range of approaches have been used to encourage participation. For example, to recruit lesbian, gay, bisexual, and transgender (LGBT) patients and health providers for their study exploring how to create culturally competent clinical settings, researchers Wilkerson, Rybicki, Barber, and Smolenski (2011) report they recruited participants by "posting fliers at LGBT-friendly businesses and community-based organizations, sending e-mails via LGBT-friendly community Listservs, and making announcements at LGBT events" (p. 379).

Recruitment efforts can also include *cultural guides*. Cultural guides, a term used in the context of culturally responsive evaluation by Frierson, Hood, Hughes, and Thomas (2010), refers to people who understand the cultural norms and experiences of the priority population. A cultural guide can be an Elder or respected person in the community, for example. Cultural guides can offer advice related to the cultural appropriateness of your approach to recruitment; assist with translating recruitment materials; discuss questions or concerns about the investigation in the participants' own language; and identify a culturally appropriate place to conduct the focus group as well as assist with other aspects of your design (i.e., focus group questions, data collection).

Incentives and Reciprocity

If participants know they will be provided an incentive or compensation before the focus group, they may be more likely to participate. Therefore, incentivizing is often beneficial for recruitment purposes (Parker & Tritter, 2006; Patton, 2015). To incentivize, researchers commonly provide gift cards to participants once the focus group is complete (Stewart & Sham-dasani, 2015). Of course, incentives can occur before, during, or through-out the entire investigation (Patton, 2015). From a culturally responsive perspective, doing something in exchange for participants' time and effort is considered a form of reciprocity. To demonstrate reciprocity, sometimes it is more appropriate to provide a service or complete a task for participants. You can volunteer your time in service to a participant's organization, for instance. The specific needs of participants, the cultural context, practical limitations (budget, time), among other things, will assist in determining the most feasible and appropriate way to reciprocate.

Number of Focus Group Participants

The optimal number of participants to include in a focus group is between six and eight (Patton, 2015; Balch & Mertens, 1999). Of course, there are practical issues that will influence the number of participants in a focus group. For example, there may be a limited number of participants that fit your sampling criteria. Or, despite your best efforts, attrition might occur. For these reasons, over-recruiting is necessary. When working with minori-tized groups, smaller focus groups may be desired particularly for discus-sions of sensitive topics. Also, if groups have been historically overlooked, a smaller focus group size may provide more time for participants to share their views, thereby making participants' voices more visible.

Ethics

For inquirers conducting focus group research, approval from an institu-tional review board is sometimes needed. This is because countless studies have subjected participants to unethical treatment by not informing par-ticipants they were participating in a study, or by deceiving participants about the purposes of a research project, resulting in harmful consequences. To protect participants and ensure they are treated ethically, institutional review boards (IRB) were created. IRBs currently exist around the world, although their scope and responsibilities may differ.

Institutional review boards. To ensure participants are treated ethically, an IRB generally requires researchers to submit their research design, including focus group protocols, participant consent forms, and information about study risks and benefits to the review committee. Because the research design submission and review process varies, researchers should locate and investigate the ethical research review process at their institution.

Professional guidelines and standards. Evaluators, in many cases, rely on professional guidelines and standards to ensure the evaluation design abides by the ethical principles set forth by their profession (see for example the American Evaluation Association's Guiding Principles For Evaluators, 2018). In addition to such guidelines, evaluators may also need to submit information about their designs and obtain approval from an ethics review committee, depending on the context of the evaluation.

Institutional review boards and professional guidelines have a significant impact on your proposed inquiry design for at least two reasons. First, they influence how your design—including the individual methods (i.e., focus groups)—will be carried out. For instance, review boards may request that you make changes to different design components, thereby altering your design. And second, institutional review boards, in particular, aim to ensure each component of your design is ethical. Therefore, they will be especially attentive to your process for gaining focus groups participants' informed consent, a topic I elaborate on below.

Informed consent. This process involves taking the time necessary to help participants understand what the study is about, discuss confidentiality issues and express any questions or concerns before they agree to participate (Barbour, 2019). Giving additional opportunities to ask questions during and after participation, emphasizing the voluntary nature of the focus group session, and letting participants know they can refuse to answer any focus group question are also aspects of informed consent. These aspects reveal how consent is continuously negotiated throughout the entire inquiry process, thereby respecting participants' decision to change their level of involvement in the investigation (Bhattacharya, 2007). Below, I offer some information commonly included in consent forms. If you desire to follow up with participants to clarify understandings, the consent form can also include language requesting permission to contact participants at a later date.

- The names and contact information of the investigators.

- A statement explaining the purpose of the study.

- The study procedures.

- Any possible risks, discomforts, and benefits.

- Information about audio/video recording. This section explains the focus group session will be audio recorded to ensure the accuracy of the transcriptions and study findings. If you plan to video record the session, this information would be provided as well.

- A statement regarding privacy and confidentiality. As noted earlier, you cannot guarantee anonymity when conducting a focus group. However, there are precautions you can take to keep the information obtained from the focus group confidential. This section outlines those precautions, noting who will have access to the focus group data and where the data will be stored. A brief discussion of codes or pseudonyms will be used once all identifying information has been removed. You may also mention whether information from the focus groups will be used for presentations or publications.

- An acknowledgment that participation is voluntary.

- Signature lines to indicate the participant has granted consent.

It is important to note that gaining informed consent from populations goes beyond addressing the components of a consent form. Informed consent requires a process that is sensitive to the literacy and linguistic diversity of participants. Furthermore, for some participants, gaining consent requires obtaining permission from a gatekeeper. Examples of gatekeepers include parents, guardians, or caregivers. For instance, in some Indigenous contexts, it is appropriate to discuss the project with and or obtain permission from Elders or respected persons before seeking consent from individuals in the community. Whatever the case, understanding how to respectfully request consent, beyond an IRB or professional guidelines, is essential to culturally responsive inquiry.

To end this chapter, I review a couple of ethical issues pertinent to focus groups that have implications for the informed consent process and how participants will negotiate their participation in your investigation. The first is related to issues of confidentiality. Because confidentiality cannot be

guaranteed within a focus group session, the risks associated with participants disclosing information that could potentially stigmatize them, jeopar-
dize their employment, cause them harm, and so on, needs to be addressed
during the consent process. Second, potential participants need to be made
aware that comments made by other focus group participants could make
them feel uncomfortable or cause stress, especially if a sensitive topic is
being discussed.

Summary

A major goal of this chapter has been to emphasize the interactive nature
of inquiry design. Relying on Maxwell and other scholars, different components of inquiry design were discussed, emphasizing how each one influences
the other. Specific design components reviewed in this chapter include inquiry purposes, theories, questions, and sampling techniques. Design options,
the appropriateness of focus groups, recruitment strategies and the number
of participants to include in a focus group were also covered. The final topic
to be discussed was ethics, focusing on institutional review boards, professional guidelines, the role of gatekeepers and how informed consent allows
participants to understand the project and change their level of involvement.

In the following chapter, we will take a close look at developing focus
group questions, facilitating focus groups, and enhancing focus group participant engagement.

References

Alatinga, K. A., & Williams, J. J. (2019). Mixed methods research for health pol-
    icy development in Africa: The case of identifying very poor households for
    health insurance premium exemptions in Ghana. *Journal of Mixed Methods
    Research, 13*(1), 69–84.

Balch, G. I., & Mertens, D. M. (1999). Focus group design and group dynamics:
    Lessons from deaf and hard of hearing participants. *American Journal of
    Evaluation, 20*(2), 265–277.

Barrett, J., & Kirk, S. (2000). Running focus groups with elderly and disabled
    elderly participants. *Applied Ergonomics, 6*, 621.

Bentz, V. M., & Shapiro, J. J. (1998). *Mindful inquiry in social research.* Thousand
    Oaks, CA: Sage.

Bhattacharya, K. (2007). Consenting to the consent form: What are the fixed and
    fluid understandings between the researcher and the researched? *Qualitative
    Inquiry, 13*(8), 1095–1115.

Bloor, M., Frankland, J. T., Thomas, M. M. & Robson, K. (2001). *Focus groups in social research.* Thousand Oaks, CA: Sage.

Bourbor, R. (2018). *Doing focus groups* (2nd ed.). Thousand Oaks, CA: Sage.

Charmaz, K. (2014). *Constructing grounded theory.* Thousand Oaks, CA: Sage.

Cox, K., Higginbotham, J., & Burton, J. (1976). Applications of focus group interviews in marketing. *Journal of Marketing, 40*(1), 77.

Denzin, N. & Lincoln, Y. (2018). *The Sage handbook of qualitative research.* Thousand Oaks, CA. Sage.

Dunbar, H., Carter, B., & Brown, J. (2018). 'Place bonding' in children's hospice care: a qualitative study. *BMJ supportive & palliative care*, bmjspcare-2018-001543.

Frierson, H. T., Hood, S., Hughes, G. B., & Thomas, V. G. (2010). Chapter 7: A guide to conducting culturally responsive evaluations. In Joy Frechtling (Ed.), *The 2010 user-friendly handbook for project evaluation* (Revision to the NSF Publication No. 02-057) (pp. 75-96). Arlington, VA: National Science Foundation.

Gaston, M. H., Porter, G. K., & Thomas, V. G. (2007). Prime time sister circles: Evaluating a gender-specific, culturally relevant health intervention to decrease major risk factors in mid-life African-American women. *Journal of the National Medical Association, 99*(4), 428–438.

Greene, J. C. (2007). *Mixed methods in social inquiry.* San Francisco, CA: John Wiley & Sons.

Greene, J. C., & Hall, J. N. (2010). Dialectics and pragmatism: Being of consequence. In A. Tashakkori & C. Teddle (Eds.), *Handbook of mixed methods in social and behavioral research* (pp. 119–144). Thousand Oaks, CA: Sage.

Halcomb, E. J., Gholizadeh, L., DiGiacomo, M., Phillips, J., & Davidson, P. M. (2007). Literature review: considerations in undertaking focus group research with culturally and linguistically diverse groups. *Journal of Clinical Nursing, 16*(6), 1000–1011.

Hall, J. N. (2010). Investigating internal accountability and collective capacity: Taking a closer look at mathematics instruction. *Journal of Curriculum and Instruction, 4*(2), 9–32.

Hall, J. N., Ahn, J., & Greene, J. C. (2012). Values-engagement in evaluation: Ideas, illustrations, and implications. *American Journal of Evaluation, 33*(2), 195–207.

Hall, J. N., & Greene, J. (Eds.). (2019). A kaleidoscope of perspectives on the potential, contributions, and grand vision of a mixed methods approach to educational inquiry (special issue). *International Journal of Research and Method in Education, 42*(3). London, UK: Routledge: Taylor & Francis Group.

House, E. R. (2017). Evaluation and the framing of race. *American Journal of Evaluation, 38*(2), 167–189.

Jabareen, Y. (2009). Building a conceptual framework: Philosophy, definitions, and procedure. *International Journal of Qualitative Methods, 8*, 49–62.

Johnson, B., & Christensen, L. (2014). *Educational research: Quantitative, qualitative, and mixed approaches* (5th ed.). Los Angeles, CA: Sage.

Kincheloe, J. L., & McLaren, P. L. (1994). Rethinking critical theory and qualitative research. In N. K. Denzin & Y. S. Lincoln (Eds.), *Handbook of qualitative research* (pp. 138–157). Thousand Oaks, CA: Sage.

Kirkhart, K. E. (2015). Unpacking the evaluator's toolbox: Observations on evaluation, privilege, equity and justice. *Evaluation Matters/He To Te Aromatawai, 1*, 7–24.

Krueger, R. A., & Casey, M. A. (2015). *Focus groups: a practical guide for applied research* (5th ed.). Thousand Oaks, CA: Sage.

Kuhn, T. (1996). *The structure of scientific revolutions* (3th ed.). Chicago: University of Chicago Press.

Madriz, E. (1998). Using focus groups with lower socioeconomic status Latina women. *Qualitative Inquiry, 4*, 114–28.

Maxwell, J. A. (2013). Research design: An interactive approach. *Social Sciences, 14*(7), 36–42.

McEntee-Atalianis, L., & Litosseliti, L. (2017). Narratives of sex-segregated professional identities. *Narrative Inquiry, 27*(1), 1–23

Merton, R., & Kendall, P. (1946). The focused interview. *American Journal of Sociology, 51*, 541–557.

Morgan, D. L. (1996). Focus groups. *Annual review of sociology, 22*(1), 129–152.

Morgan, D. L. (2007). Paradigms lost and pragmatism regained: Methodological implications of combining qualitative and quantitative methods. *Journal of Mixed Methods Research, 1*(1), 48–76.

Morgan, D. L. (2019). *Basic and advanced focus groups.* Thousand Oaks, CA: Sage.

Munje, P. N. (2019). The impact of teacher professional conduct on learner experiences and performance in poor school communities in South Africa. *Compare: A Journal of Comparative and International Education, 49*(4), 511–528.

Newmann, F. M., King, M. B., and Rigdon, M. (1997). Accountability and school performance: Implications from restructuring schools. *Harvard Educational Review, 67*(1), 41–69.

O'Carroll, A., & Wainwright, D. (2019). Making sense of street chaos: an ethnographic exploration of homeless people's health service utilization. *International Journal for Equity in Health, 18*(1), 113.

Parker, A., & Tritter, J. (2006). Focus group method and methodology: Current practice and recent debate. *International Journal of Research & Method in Education, 29*(1), 23–37.

Patton, M. Q. (2015). *Qualitative evaluation and research methods.* Thousand Oaks, CA: Sage.

Pollack, S. (2003). Focus-group methodology in research with incarcerated women: Race, power, and collective experience. *Affilia, 18*, 461–472.

Power, C. B., & Allaman, E. (2012). *How participatory action research can promote social change and help youth development: Report 2013-10.* Harvard, MA: Berkman Center Research Publication.

Prasad, P. (2018). *Crafting qualitative research: Beyond positivist traditions.* (2nd ed.). New York, NY: Routledge.

Prince, H., Nadin, S., Crow, M., Maki, L., Monture, L., Smith, J., & Kelley, M. L. (2019). "If you understand you cope better with it": The role of education in building palliative care capacity in four First Nations communities in Canada. *BMC public health, 19*(1), 768.

Robinson, A., Davis, M., Hall, J. N., Lauckner, C., & Anderson, A. (2019). It takes an e-village: Supporting black mothers in sustaining breastfeeding through Facebook communities, *Journal of Human Lactation, 35*(3), 569–582.

Roulston, K. (2010). *Reflective interviewing: A guide to theory and practice.* Thousand Oaks, CA: Sage.

Ryan, K., Ganda, T., Culbertson, M., & Carlson, C. (2013). Focus groups evidence: Implications for design and analysis. *American Journal of Evaluation, 35*(3), 328–345.

Schwandt, T. (1989). Solutions to the paradigm controversy: Coping with uncertainty. *Journal of Contemporary Ethnography, 17*(4), 379–407.

Sharp, B. K. (2019). Stress as experienced by people with dementia: An interpretative phenomenological analysis. *Dementia, 18*(4), 1427–1445.

Singletary, G. (2019). Beyond PTSD: Black male fragility in the context of trauma. *Journal of Aggression, Maltreatment & Trauma,* 1–20.

Smith, J. A., Flowers, P., & Larkin, M. (2009). *Interpretative phenomenological analysis: Theory, method and research.* London: Sage

Stake, R. (1995). *The art of case study research.* Thousand Oaks, CA: Sage.

Stewart, D. W., & Shamdasani, P. (2015). *Focus groups: Theory and practice* (3rd ed.). Thousand Oaks, CA: Sage.

Tavallaei, M., & Talib, M. A. (2010). A general perspective on the role of theory in qualitative research. *Journal of International Social Research, 3*(11), 570–577.

Wilkerson, J. M., Rybicki, S., Barber, C. A., & Smolenski, D. J. (2011). Creating a culturally competent clinical environment for LGBT patients. *Journal of Gay & Lesbian Social Services, 23*(3), 376–394.

Wilkinson, S. (1999). Focus groups: A feminist method. *Psychology of Women Quarterly, 23*(2), 221–244.

Van Maanen, J. (2011). *Tales from the field: on writing ethnography* (2nd ed.). Chicago: University of Chicago Press.

Yin, R. K. (2011). *Applications of case study research.* Thousand Oaks, CA: Sage.

CHAPTER THREE

Focus Group Protocol Development, Engaging Participants, and the Moderator's Role

In This Chapter

- Focus Group Protocol Development

- Organizing Your Focus Group Protocol

- Question Development Fundamentals

- Engaging Focus Group Participants

- Pre-Focus Group Questionnaire

- Before, During, and After the Focus Group

- Moderator's Role

- Moderator as Research Instrument and Agent for Change

- Summary

I N THIS CHAPTER, I review how to develop a focus group protocol pointing out different protocol formats and how to organize your protocol content. I also offer different types of focus group questions and fundamental aspects related to qualitative interviewing. Then, I discuss how including "focusing exercises" can serve to enhance participant engagement and cultural responsiveness (Bloor et al., 2001). Other topics covered in this chapter include the purpose of a pre-focus group questionnaire, tips to keep in mind before, during, and after the focus group as well as how the moderator's role is understood in relation to qualitative research and the culturally responsive stance advanced in this book.

Focus Group Protocol Development

The *focus group protocol* is sometimes referred to as a focus group interview guide. Whichever term is used, it reflects your plan for how you will engage focus group participants. Developing your focus group protocol requires that you decide the overall structure or format used for the focus group, topics and issues covered, and specific questions and probes. Any activities or focusing exercises (described below) planned for the focus group session will also need to be determined. However, focus group protocol development should begin after inquiry purposes and questions have been articulated (Stewart & Shamdasani, 2015). This ensures the necessary topics are covered during the focus group discussion to address your inquiry questions and participants' concerns. That said, it is important to note that not every aspect of the focus group discussion can be predicted in advance. This is because focus groups, like your design, are lively and dynamic; participants can take the questions in several unanticipated directions. Even the most well developed focus group protocol will not reflect exactly how the focus group will happen. Despite this, a focus group protocol is still necessary and valuable, affording a systematic procedure for data collection.

When developing a focus group protocol, one of the first decisions to be made concerns the general format. There are three common focus group protocol formats: (1) structured, (2) semi-structured, and (3) informal.

Structured format. Focus group protocols that use a *structured* format include questions that are investigator-centric. This means many of the questions are specific to the inquirer's agenda or inquiry topic. Structured focus groups, then, do not give enough room for participants to guide the discussion or introduce new topics (Bloor et al., 2001). As a result, the structured format may not stimulate conversation among participants because "group members concentrate on responding to the questions of the facilitator" (Bloor et al., 2001, p. 47).

Semi-structured format. The *semi-structured* protocol format balances broad and specific topic-related questions. This format permits inquirers to pursue their line of inquiry, but is more flexible as it allows participants to introduce new topics or issues during the discussion.

Unstructured format. An *unstructured* focus group protocol includes few, if any, predetermined questions. Therefore, it is the most responsive format, granting participants more control over the focus group session.

Organizing Your Focus Group Protocol

Once you have decided on the format for your focus group protocol, you will need to organize the content. Protocol content is often organized around three broad categories of questions: (1) warm-up questions, (2) questions related to the inquiry topics and participant issues, and (3) closing questions.

Warm-Up Questions. Warm-up questions orient each participant to others in the group and establish an environment where participants feel at ease interacting as a group (Krueger & Casey, 2015; Morgan, 2019). Warm-up questions are not about the research topic. Rather, these questions are easy to answer and of interest to the group (Morgan, 2019). To kick off the focus group and get everyone talking, it is common to ask participants warm-up questions during participant introductions. See the *Before the Focus Group* section below for more discussion on this same point.

Questions Related to the Topics Covered. This section will include the key topics and issues addressed during the focus groups and the specific questions used to address each topic. The topics and questions included on the protocol will be thoughtfully informed by your inquiry design components (i.e., purposes, questions, and theories). Much of your time developing the protocol will be spent on this section, as the bulk of the focus group protocol will consist of these questions. However, in contrast to an individual interview protocol, a focus group protocol covers fewer topics and questions, allowing all focus group participants an opportunity to share. Although it is challenging to say with certainty how many questions to include on a focus group protocol, most protocols include approximately a dozen questions (Stewart & Shamdasani, 2015).

A common way to organize what you want to cover in your protocol is to begin with broad questions followed by specific questions. This way of arranging your questions is characterized as the 'funnel' approach (Stewart & Shamdasani, 2015). Asking broad questions first allows you to cast a wide net, generating ideas, and attitudes about a topic to be explored later in the focus group. Such broad questions are referred to as *grand-tour* or "uncued" questions (Morgan, 2019, p. 65); they can help facilitate additional conversation among the participants. Grand-tour questions are particularly purposeful to elicit information when little is known about a topic, concept, or term, which can often be the case when discussing topics with hard-to-reach or marginalized communities. The advantage of a grand tour question such as, *What are examples of the drinks your child consumes on a typical day?* is that it can provide information you did not previously have in mind. Also, the general information afforded by grand tour questions can serve as a foundation to delve deeply or funnel down into topics and issues with more specific questions (Krueger & Casey, 2015; Morgan, 2019).

In addition to grand tour questions, other types of questions can be used to cover inquiry topics and relevant participant issues. Patton (2015) describes question types that can accommodate any topic and stimulate conversation among participants. The first type, *experience and behavior* questions, provides information related to a specific event or experience. For this type of question, you are trying to elicit a descriptive story rather than general comments. An example of this type of question would be something like, *Please walk me through how you identify healthy drinks while at the grocery store.* Another type of question, *comparison/contrast questions*, asks participants to think about a situation, place, group of people, or a person, and draw comparisons between them. *How is your experience deciding which beverages to serve your family now that you've completed the Healthy Beverage Workshop?* is an example of this type of question. Opinion and feeling questions are other types of questions available to explore your topic of interest. *Opinion* questions such as, *What do you think about the nutrition expert's recommendation to drink no more than one sugary beverage per day?* are useful to ask when you want to know what people think about a situation. *Feeling* questions such as, *How do you feel when your children refuse to drink the healthy beverages you serve them?* seek to understand participants' emotions (fear, happiness, disgust, surprise).

Closing Questions. This section of the focus group protocol includes questions valuable to summarize significant points made during the focus group and elicit information that was not covered during the focus group (Liamputtong, 2011). One type of closing question is a *summary question*; it is asked after a brief overview of the discussion is provided (Krueger & Casey, 2015). For this type of closing, you might say something like, *During the focus group, I noticed several themes. These included (XYZ).* After your oral overview of the themes, the moderator could then ask, *Do you think I summarized those themes correctly?*

Another type of closing question is referred to as an *insurance* question because it gives a chance for the participant to add information that has not been mentioned, ensuring critical aspects of the topic have been covered (Krueger & Casey, 2015). For this type of question, a moderator might ask, *Though I have asked many questions of you, I want to allow you to share with me anything that you would like to add. Is there anything else you would like to share?*

From a culturally responsive perspective, bringing closure to the focus group also includes thanking participants for their time: *I want to thank you for sharing your experiences with me today. I really appreciated your insights and time.* As part of your closing, you may also want to ask if it is fine to follow up with any additional questions—*If I have any follow up questions later, may I contact you again?*

Question Development Fundamentals

When developing questions for focus group protocol, there are some fundamental aspects to keep in mind. These include asking open-ended questions, probing for clarification, asking one question at a time, asking clear questions, and avoiding leading questions.

Ask Open-Ended Questions. You want to avoid dichotomous questions because they can simply be answered with a yes-or-no response and are not apt to generate further description (Stewart & Shamdasani, 2015) (e.g., *Do you enjoy working with the new teachers at your school? Does your principal provide relevant professional development opportunities?*). Instead, ask open-ended questions. Open-ended questions provoke participants to respond with a story (e.g., *Tell me what it is like working with new teachers at your school.*).

Probe for Clarification and Elaboration. While avoiding dichotomous questions is an established qualitative principle, there are occasions when they can be used (Morgan, 2019). For example, if you find it necessary to include a dichotomous question on your protocol such as, *Does your principal offer professional development opportunities that are relevant?*, follow up on the question with *probes*. If the participant says yes, then use a probe such as: *If so, how are the professional development activities related to your job?* If the participant replies no, follow up by asking a question such as *What could the principal do to make professional development experiences more relevant?* However, probing is not restricted to dichotomous question follow-up. Probing is also a powerful strategy to have participants further elaborate on any question. For instance, protocols can include probing questions such as *I heard you say [X]. Can you provide an example of [X]?*

Ask One Question at a Time. While the advice to ask one question at a time may seem obvious, it's common for focus group protocols to include a question like, *What are the strengths and challenges of the program?* If you want to improve your data quality, asking one question at a time (in this case asking about program strengths and weaknesses separately) is the better route to go.

Ask Clear Questions. As the inquirer, you have the responsibility to ask understandable questions. Do not place the burden on your participants to figure out what you are asking (Patton, 2015). To ask clear questions, keep questions short as lengthy questions tend to be confusing; also, avoid using jargon, as participants who are not experts may be unfamiliar with those terms (Krueger & Casey, 2015).

Avoid Asking Leading Questions. Qualitative interviewing requires the moderator to resist asking leading questions. As Morgan (2019) points out

> leading questions emphasize the researcher's perspective and thus begin the discussion by moving the participants in a direction influenced by the researcher. It is better to spend some time considering how the participants experience and think about the topic and then ask about it from their standpoint (p. 64)

An additional fundamental aspect of focus group protocol development is arranging your protocol is to include transition sentences. The transition sentences are needed more so for the focus group participants. They help participants follow the sequence, or order, of topics covered during the focus group discussion. For example, to assist participants with transitioning from one topic to the next, you might use a transition sentence such as, *Now that you've had a chance to think about what you and your children drink on a typical day, I'd like to discuss what influences the types of beverages you and your family choose to drink.* Hearing such oral cues will enable focus group participants to follow the shift from one topic to the next during the discussion.

A final fundamental aspect to consider when developing a focus group protocol concerns question sequencing. Here, the format of your focus group protocol will determine the extent to which you can sequence questions. For instance, the structured focus group format provides the most flexibility when sequencing questions as the questions are predetermined (Patton, 2015). Patton (2015) and Stewart & Shamdasani (2015) offer some general advice for sequencing questions.

- Begin with more recent events, then ask questions about earlier experiences.

- Discuss easy, less controversial topics before moving on to more complicated or controversial issues.

- Place questions of most importance near the top of the protocol, and least important questions closer to the end.

- Move from more general questions to more specific questions.

While sequencing questions based on the general advice offered above is worthwhile, it is also helpful to remember that focus group participants may not discuss topics in the order presented on your protocol; therefore, flexibility is needed to shift the sequence of topics in response to participants' concerns and avoid missing generative insights (Barbour, 2018).

Engaging Focus Group Participants

As you continue to reflect on your focus group protocol, think about how you will encourage the participants to interact with each other. Over the years, I've found activities or what Bloor et al. (2001) refer to as *focusing exercises* fruitful to promote participant engagement. Adding a focusing exercise to your protocol also gives some variety to your focus group session. As you continue to develop your focus group protocol, review the list of focusing exercises below, thinking carefully about how one or a variation of one might fit the cultural context and goals of your investigation.

Ranking. In ranking exercises, participants are provided with statements related to the phenomena of interest and then asked to rank them in order of importance (Barbour, 2018). The results from this focusing exercise can be useful to glean insights into the most prominent domains, solutions, or meanings of the group.

Vignettes. Short stories or *vignettes* detail a hypothetical scenario (Barbour, 2018). After being presented with a written vignette, focus group participants are invited to respond to the scenario. Health researchers have found this technique advantageous when conducting focus groups in marginalized communities such as among older adults (over 64 years old) (Brondani, MacEntee, Bryant, & O'Neill, 2008). Colucci (2007) suggests "scenarios can be particularly useful to investigate stereotypes and ways in which participants would behave in a specific circumstance" (i.e., a peer who disclosed suicidal thoughts) (p. 1427).

Free listings. This activity invites participants to verbally list characteristics of a domain or solution to a problem while the moderator records participants' ideas (via a flip chart or whiteboard). Alternatively, participants could individually write their responses on paper and then report their answers to the group (Colucci, 2007).

Rating. For this activity, participants respond to something (word, object, or picture) that must be rated on a scale. After participants share their ratings, the moderators ask them to discuss their rationales for the ratings they provided. Referencing Krueger (1998), Colucci (2007) makes clear the focus of the rating activity is the discussion generated from the rating, rather than the rating itself. This means that the analysis of the focus group discussion emphasizes participants' perspectives—not their scores. This focusing exercise was valuable for discussing a sensitive topic (suicide prevention) with youths from different cultures (India, Italy, and Australia) (Colucci, 2007). As a result of asking participants to rate the effectiveness of suicide prevention strategies on a 5-point Likert-type scale, with 1 representing *not effective at all*, 3 representing *sometimes effective*, and 5 representing *very effective*, Colucci (2007) was able to compare similarities and difference across cultures in the discussion that resulted, reiterating here that the comparison is not across scores, but about the discussion generated by the activity.

Pile sorting. This activity requires participants to sort cards into groups according to how the elements represented on the cards relate to or are different from each other (Colucci, 2007). The cards can be actual cards, paper, or other items such as pictures or photographs. The moderator can have the categories for the sorting activity predetermined, based on a review of relevant literature. One possible result of providing categories for pile sorting is that a participant may not perceive a card to fit neatly into one of the predetermined categories. Another option, then, is to have participants decide the categories for sorting the cards. Both approaches to pile sorting have the potential to generate meaningful insights if the moderator asks follow-up questions, inquiring about the participants' decision-making while card sorting.

Other Options for Focus Group Participant Engagement. According to Colucci (2007), other options well suited to engaging focus group participants who may have hesitancy discussing a sensitive topic include (1) having participants draw a picture in response to a question posed by the moderator; (2) having participants create a collage with materials (i.e., magazines); (3) distributing a sentence related to the topic for participants to complete; (4) allowing participants to present an object (favorite stuffed animal, trophy) during the focus group in response to a prompt provided prior to the focus group; and (5) inviting participants to role-play a situation. Photo-elicitation is yet another option to enhance participant engagement. See the case example, Box 5.2. *Photo Elicitation Focus Groups with Older Adults*, in Chapter 5 for an explanation of this technique and how it was used with adults over the age of 65.

Moderators have the option to use more than one exercise during a focus group. Of course, decisions about whether to incorporate one or multiple focusing exercises are determined by the purpose of the investigation, duration of the focus group meeting (i.e., one hour), number of focus groups (one session or multiple meetings), and participant characteristics (i.e., age, reading and writing skills) among other things (Bloor et al., 2001; Colucci, 2007). Moreover, investigators will need to decide the placement of the focusing exercise in their focus group. For instance, focusing exercises can be included at the beginning of a focus group as a type of warm-up activity (see Appendix A: Sample Focus Group Protocol, for example) in the middle of a focus group to briefly change the structure of an otherwise conventional focus group session, or at the end of a focus group session to review, clarify or summarize salient points made during the focus group session (Colucci, 2007). Finally, while focusing exercises can foster discussion and lead to sharing of deeper cultural meanings, it is difficult to foresee how participants will react (Liamputtong, 2011). Therefore, attending to participants' responses is necessary to ensure positive outcomes and to capitalize on the potential of the focusing exercise (Barbour, 2018; Liamputtong, 2011). See Chapter 5 for further discussion on the use of focusing exercises with youth and older adults.

Pre-Focus Group Questionnaire

Preparing for your focus group may also involve collecting demographic information or other data relevant to the study to ensure participants meet the selection criteria. Depending on the investigation, it might be useful to gather this information in the form of a pre-focus group questionnaire. In contrast to quantitative questionnaires, a pre-focus group questionnaire is more qualitative in nature and includes a short set of closed- and/or open-ended questions. Because they are short, pre-focus group questionnaires can be completed just before the focus group begins. For instance, just before their focus groups, designed to inform the development of an intervention for pregnant women who are low-income and overweight, Thomas et al., (2014) had participants complete a pre-focus group questionnaire. The short questionnaire was designed to capture demographic and health-related information. The demographic questions asked about the women's racial/ethnic identities, ages, and body mass indexes. Other questions inquired about the context of each woman's current pregnancy (planned, unplanned) as well as anxieties about gaining weight during pregnancy. Here, we can see how, in addition to screening participants, a pre-focus group questionnaire provides valuable information to further contextualize focus group data. Furthermore, using a pre-focus group questionnaire for short-answer or closed-ended questions maintains the open-ended nature of the focus group. Moreover, a pre-questionnaire allows the inquirer an additional pathway to capture potentially sensitive information (i.e., person's health, socioeconomic status, age) in a manner that is more comfortable for focus group participants.

After the focus group protocol has been reviewed and/or piloted (see Chapter 4 discussion on piloting), and participants have provided their informed consent (see Chapter 2 discussion on informed consent), you will conduct the focus group at the agreed upon time and location. In the following sections, I offer some recommendations with examples to consider before, during, and after the focus group. I then conclude the chapter with a close examination of the moderator's role.

Before the Focus Group

Before the focus group session, the moderator welcomes everyone. Welcoming focus group participants is not a trivial matter as the process serves to establish trust with participants. During the welcome, the moderator introduces herself and the note taker. Although participants have already consented to participate in the focus group, moderators also provide time before the focus group to review the consent form, reminding participants about the study procedures, risks and benefits, incentives for participation, audio/video recording procedures, privacy issues and so on. After welcoming everyone to the focus group, the moderator explains the rules of engagement. Reviewing the rules of engagement ensures participants show respect toward others' views during the focus group discussion. Also, before focus group questions are asked, it is customary to have participants introduce themselves. Inviting participants to say something about themselves (i.e., their hobby) or participate in a warm-up activity gets participants talking early on in the discussion and builds rapport (Liamputtong, 2011). Be sure to ask participants to clearly state their names or how they wish to be identified during introductions (real name, pseudonym). Having this information recorded will serve as a point of reference to identify speakers when transcribing the focus group session (Bloor et al., 2001). Review Appendix

A: Sample Focus Group Protocol to see how the sections (welcome, intro-ductions/warm-up, ground rules, etc.) have been incorporated into a focus group protocol.

During and After the Focus Group

Making mention of participants' names throughout the focus group, such as in "*I appreciate your points made, Juan*" is not only respectful but also provides additional points of reference to identify individual speakers on the recording (Bloor et al., 2001). Other methods for identifying particular par-ticipants following the focus group include having them identify themselves in a particular order (clockwise) and mapping the room and the orientation of each participant for future review alongside the audio recording.

After the focus group session, take a moment to check your recording device to ensure the data were recorded, collect any notes taken, and jot down the duration of the focus group for your records (Patton, 2015). Also, be sure to write down your thoughts, questions or concerns once the session is complete (Patton, 2015).

Moderator's Role

As mentioned in Chapter 1, the role of a moderator is to facilitate a collec-tive conversation *among* participants, which requires several skills. Also, it is important to recognize how working as a qualitative and culturally responsive inquirer positions the moderator's role. Accordingly, in what fol-lows, I first discuss key facilitation skills needed to moderate a focus group. Then, building on that discussion, I take a slightly broader perspective, con-sidering the moderator's role as a research instrument from a qualitative perspective, and agent for change from a culturally responsive stance.

Facilitation skills. The effectiveness of any focus group is heavily reliant on the moderator's facilitation skills. A key skill required of moderators is to be a good listener (Liamputtong, 2011). This means paying attention to what participants are saying in a manner that signals you are genuinely interested in what they are sharing (Morgan, 2019). Moderators also need to be nonjudgmental (Liamputtong, 2011). This refers to moderators not signaling (i.e., head nodding) their approval or disapproval. Being nonjudgmental allows you to hear the range of diverse opinions and perspectives offered by the group (Morgan, 2019). Withholding judgment is especially important when discussing a sensitive issue or conducting a focus group with underrepresented groups whose voices are seldom heard. Moderators should also be cautious of sharing their personal opinions as this could signal judgment or stifle the discussion (Krueger & Casey, 2015). However, if a moderator discloses information about her own experiences related to the topic, it could encourage participants to disclose their own information (Liamputtong, 2011). Other moderator competencies include engaging participants who are hesitant to speak or haven't had a chance to share. For example, moderators may need to tactfully draw participants into the conversation using prompts such as, [Name of participant], *I see you're shaking your head in agreement. Would you like to share your thoughts?* Also, moderators will need to determine when to provide additional time for participants to respond or if a break (i.e., snack) is needed (Krueger & Casey, 2015).

Moderating also entails skillfully attending to and capturing verbal and nonverbal cues of the participants (see Chapter 8 for more detail). Meaningfully attending to participants' perspectives may require a co-facilitator. Having another person work with you to conduct a focus group helps to make certain that all the topics have been covered during the discussion. For example, in one situation, I was primarily responsible for conducting the focus group and the co-facilitator was a content knowledge expert responsible for asking follow-up questions or clarifying information when needed. This joint facilitation worked well, especially when participants raised specific concerns about the content (the nutrition policy) that I was unable to address. In another case, I co-facilitated a focus group with small children (Freeman & Hall, 2012). Art supplies were provided so that children could complete a focusing exercise. Managing food, markers, paper, and the dynamics of the children themselves was much easier with two moderators. These examples illustrate the point that joint facilitation can be responsive to participants' needs depending on the context.

In terms of capturing verbal information, there are two things to note. First, on occasion, cultural responsiveness in a specific context means conducting the focus group in participants' local language. If the moderator is not fluent in the participants' language, identifying someone who can conduct the focus group in the language of participants is recommended (Krueger & Casey, 2015). Second, to capture verbal information moderators often rely on technology. However, technology can fail. Recordings can get destroyed or recorders can decide not to work. Should the audio recording not work, for whatever reason, notes serve as a safeguard, ensuring you have aspects of the focus group session documented. Because of this, the role of the note taker becomes even more imperative. Furthermore, the note taker role is invaluable, as this person makes certain key quotes, important discussion points, and participants' nonverbal cues are captured.

Moderator as Research Instrument and Agent for Change

Qualitative researchers and program evaluators who use qualitative methods recognize that being a moderator is more than merely facilitating a discussion between people. In qualitative research, the moderator is understood as a research instrument.

Moderator as Research Instrument. The role of the moderator as a research instrument implies that as a moderator facilitates a focus group, her cultural background, sensitivity to the topic, relationship to the participants, and competencies interact with the generated data, hindering and/or advancing the goals of the investigation. And, as a result, the moderator, as a research instrument, affects focus group data quality. Understanding yourself as a research instrument, then, means being aware of the influence your position, abilities, and characteristics have on the focus group process. Furthermore, the notion of a moderator as a research instrument acknowledges the role you and your focus group questions play in co-constructing knowledge with your participants (Lahman et al., 2011; Rodriguez et al., 2011). Even if the participants are highly interactive and primarily discuss topics among themselves, you, as the moderator, contribute to the co-construction of the focus group conversation by, among other things, asking questions and probing for clarification. Finally, functioning in the role of an instrument means accepting that moderating is not "simply voyeuristic but serves a purpose" (Xu & Storr, 2012, p. 14). As culturally responsive moderators, this purpose is to advance social justice, serving as an agent for change.

Agents for Change. Recall, in Chapter 1, the core assumptions of the culturally responsive stance put forward in this book treat focus groups as sites for social justice. In this regard, beyond the role of research instrument, culturally responsive moderators perceive themselves as *agents for change*, responsible for engaging the power and privilege inherent in social relations and creating spaces for meaningful interactions and story sharing (Rodriguez, Schwartz, Lahman, & Geist, 2011). Engaging power and privilege as an agent for change involves asking questions that challenge assumptions about marginalized groups, and engaging how systems of dominance intersect with individual identities and institutions. In short, a culturally responsive focus group moderator attempts to question the status quo. Of course, what questioning the status quo means, and how it is accomplished within the context of a focus group, vary based on the cultural context. The point I want to reinforce here is that culturally responsive moderators use focus groups to negotiate, resist, and/or even transform systems of dominance. This does not mean that culturally responsive moderators do not recognize or ask about the constraints and oppressive structures within which participants are embedded. On the contrary, culturally responsive moderators acknowledge these restrictions, but also treat the participants themselves as active instruments, capable of addressing some of the challenges (albeit in their own unique ways) associated with their cultural context. Moreover, viewing focus groups as sites of social justice is essential to center participants' narratives and counterbalance dominant narratives that describe the culture of marginalized communities as "problematic" or "deficient."

Moderator Characteristics. A final point to be made is that some culturally responsive qualitative researchers and evaluators posit that the ability of moderators to comprehend participants' cultural cues increases when they share similar lived experiences (Frierson, Hood, Hughes, & Thomas, 2001), particularly when they share characteristics related to gender or race (Morgan, 2019). While "moderator matching" (Morgan, 2019) may be ideal, there are times when it is not feasible (Frierson, Hood, Hughes, & Thomas, 2010). Furthermore, as Thomas (2004) rightly reminds us, moderator matching does not guarantee cultural responsiveness. Put differently, cultural responsiveness does not rely on shared lived experiences or matching social identities alone. Cultural responsiveness demands that moderators act respectfully toward participants and address inequalities.

Summary

A key purpose of this chapter was to assist you in planning your focus group. Recommendations and examples were offered throughout the chapter to guide the development of your focus group protocol, a vital and necessary tool for conducting culturally responsive, systematic, and effective focus groups. I have given an overview of formatting options to organize your protocol, question types, and strategies for engaging participants, as well as explained the multiple demands of the moderator's role, including the skills needed to facilitate focus groups, and responsibilities as a research instrument and an agent for change.

The significance of focus group planning and preparation cannot be overemphasized as it has direct implications for capturing cultural insights and the quality of the focus group data produced, the subject of the next of Chapter 4.

References

Barbour, R. (2018). *Doing focus groups*. London. Sage.

Bloor, M., Frankland, J., Thomas, M., and Robson, K. (Eds.). (2001). *Focus groups in social research*. Thousand Oaks, CA: Sage.

Brondani, M. A., MacEntee, M. I., Bryant, S. R., & O'Neill, B. (2008). Using written vignettes in focus groups among older adults to discuss oral health as a sensitive topic. *Qualitative Health Research, 18*(8), 1145–1153.

Colucci, E. (2007). "Focus groups can be fun": The use of activity-oriented questions in focus group discussions. *Qualitative health research, 17*(10), 1422–1433.

Freeman, M., & Hall, J. N. (2012). The complexity of practice: Participant observation and values-engagement in a responsive evaluation of a professional development school partnership. *American Journal of Evaluation, 33*(4), 483–495.

Frierson, H. T, Hood, S., Hughes, G. B., & Thomas, V. G. (2010). Chapter 7: A guide to conducting culturally responsive evaluations. In Joy Frechtling (Ed.), *The 2010 user-friendly handbook for project evaluation (Revision to NSF Publication No. 02-057)* (pp. 75–96). Arlington, VA: National Science Foundation.

Krueger, R. A. & Casey, M. A. (2015). *Focus groups: A Practical Guide for Applied Research* (5th ed.). Thousand Oaks, CA: Sage.

Lahman, M. K., Geist, M. R., Rodriguez, K. L., Graglia, P., & DeRoche, K. K. (2011). Culturally responsive relational reflexive ethics in research: The three Rs. *Quality & quantity, 45*(6), 1397–1414.

Liamputtong, P. (2011). *Focus group methodology: Principle and practice*. Thousand Oaks, CA: Sage.

Morgan, D. (2019). *Basic and advanced focus groups.* Thousand Oaks, CA: Sage.

Patton, M. Q. (2015). *Qualitative evaluation and research methods.* Thousand Oaks, CA: Sage.

Rodriguez, K. L., Schwartz, J. L., Lahman, M. K., & Geist, M. R. (2011). Culturally responsive focus groups: Reframing the research experience to focus on participants. *International Journal of Qualitative Methods, 10*(4), 400–417.

Stewart, D. W., & Shamdasani, P. (2015). *Focus groups: Theory and practice* (3rd ed.). Thousand Oaks, CA: Sage.

Thomas, M., Vieten, C., Adler, N., Ammondson, I., Coleman-Phox, K., Epel, E., & Laraia, B. (2014). Potential for a stress reduction intervention to promote healthy gestational weight gain: Focus groups with low-income pregnant women. *Women's Health Issues, 24*(3), e305–e311.

Xu, M. A., & Storr, G. B. (2012). Learning the concept of researcher as instrument in qualitative research. *The Qualitative Report, 17*(Art. 42), 1–18. Retrieved from http://www.nova.edu/ssss/QR/QR17/storr.pdf4

CHAPTER FOUR

Establishing Culturally Responsive Focus Group Quality

In This Chapter

- Multicultural Validity

- Inquirer Reflexivity

T HIS CHAPTER TACKLES THE question of quality in culturally responsive focus group research. I use the word "tackle" intentionally, because questions about quality in qualitative research and focus group research remain unsettled. While social science inquirers agree quality inquiry is necessary to advance scientific knowledge, there are different conceptualizations about *what* constitutes quality inquiry and *how* it is achieved. To be sure, numerous guidelines, criteria, and standards exist for researchers and evaluators to ensure excellent qualitative work (Cypress, 2017; Frierson, Hood, Hughes, & Thomas, 2010; Kirkhart, 1995, 2005, 2010; Lincoln & Guba, 1985). However, as Tracey (2010) rightly points out, "values for quality, like all social knowledge, are ever-changing and situated within local contexts and current conversations" (p. 837). With Tracey's (2010) point in mind, this chapter is considered part of a larger conversation on quality; therefore, it represents only one view on how to establish culturally responsive focus groups—not the only view.

Before delving into the perspective on quality advanced in this chapter, and how it can be achieved, I want to take a moment to make a few points. First, culturally responsive inquirers do not assess the quality of their focus group design *after* their project is complete. Rather, it is incumbent upon culturally responsive inquirers to plan how quality will be addressed throughout the research, and to continually assess the implementation of their focus group design as well as determine the quality of their design in hindsight (Cypress, 2017).

Second, my perspective on quality emphasizes two central concepts: validity and inquirer reflexivity. I selected these concepts because they are emphasized within the evaluation and qualitative research communities as critical to the quality of any inquiry (Freeman, deMarrais, Preissle, Roulston, & St. Pierre, 2007; Kirkhart, 1995, 2010). Third, the conceptualization of validity and inquirer reflexivity presented in this chapter is informed by the culturally responsive evaluation literature (Kirkhart, 1995, 2010). This conceptualization of validity can accommodate the goals of qualitative research and focus group inquiry. Also, I view validity and inquirer reflexivity as theorized in culturally responsive evaluation practice congruent with the notion of cultural responsiveness described in this book and appropriate to tackle the quality of culturally responsive focus groups. Fourth, it is acknowledged that the term "validity" has an ingrained Eurocentric framing as well as a historical link to the tradition of positivism. Recognizing these issues, I borrow Kirkhart's (1995) notion of *multicultural validity* to discuss validity in this chapter.

Multicultural Validity

Quality refers to the trustworthiness of inquiry, or the extent to which readers can have confidence in the results of your culturally responsive focus group design (Cypress, 2017). One common criterion for establishing inquiry quality is *validity*. In qualitative research, validity refers to "data appropriateness, which makes it possible to provide an accurate account of the experiences of participants within and beyond the immediate context" (Spiers, Morse, Olson, Mayan & Barrett, 2018, p. 1). Although there are issues associated with the term validity, as mentioned earlier, multicultural validity (Kirkhart, 1995, 2010), in my assessment, addresses these concerns. That is, Kirkhart's (1995) use of the term, *multicultural* alongside *validity* reframes the traditional notion of validity by drawing attention to the fact that validity is both multifaceted and culturally situated. To be clear, her use of the term "multicultural validity" is not to argue for a new form of validity. Rather, Kirkhart's point is to assert that validity does not exist "outside cultural context because validity resides in the applications and the applications are always culturally imbedded" (Kirkhart, 2010, p. 401). *Multicultural validity*, then, refers to the inquirer's ability to generate trustworthy inferences based on the culturally responsive implementation of design components (Kirkhart, 1995, 2010).

So, how can you, as a culturally responsive inquirer, use multicultural validity to enhance the quality of your focus group design? Kirkhart (1995, 2010) provides a framework that operationalizes four dimensions of multicultural validity to assist inquirers in applying design components in culturally sensitive ways. These include (1) theoretical, (2) methodological, (3) interpersonal, and (4) consequential validity (Kirkhart, 1995, 2010). The validity dimensions are distinct but also interrelated. Admittedly, the framework does not represent *every* aspect of multicultural validity. That said, it does center participants' cultural context, and acknowledges how power differentials privilege some cultural values, perspectives, identities, and experiences over others (Kirkhart, 2010). In the next section, I briefly outline the dimensions of multicultural validity and how they can be achieved. For further details, you are highly encouraged to read Kirkhart's (1995, 2010) scholarship on multicultural validity. Also, see Chapter 5, Box 5.1 *I don't understand the question?": Focus groups with transnational migrant newcomer youth in evaluation* for a case example illustrating how evaluators applied multicultural validity to their focus groups with youth.

Theoretical Validity. This dimension concerns the culturally responsive application of theory to inquiry. As discussed in Chapter 2, theories applied to focus groups can include conceptual frameworks (i.e., phenomenon-specific theory), paradigms (abstract, philosophical theory) and their associated perspectives. Before applying theories to focus groups, Kirkhart (2010) advises assessing their cultural congruence by addressing the following (p. 403):

1. Notice who the authors are and explore their background, location, training, experience, and personal characteristics.

2. Examine the process of theory development.

3. Consider the time period in which the theory was developed and/or came to prominence.

4. Notice whether the theory assumes an implicit *strength* or *deficit* model of the phenomenon of interest.

5. Consider how the theory positions the evaluator in relation to those who are evaluated—either as program providers or consumers.

6. Notice the theorist's use of language, symbolism, and metaphor.

7. Notice the scope of attention to culture.

8. Consider the epistemologies underlying theoretical positions.

9. Consider both what's included in a particular theory vs. what is not addressed.

Although Kirkhart (2010) discusses theoretical validity in the context of evaluation, the aspects of theory that she argues we examine are relevant for qualitative inquirers as well. To be clear, the point here is that theories themselves are culturally embedded (Kirkhart, 2010). Therefore, it becomes imperative for inquirers to understand the cultural context of theories and assess the extent to which theories are relevant for a particular cultural group, before deciding to apply them to focus groups.

Methodological Validity. This dimension concerns assessments of the cultural appropriateness of the overall inquiry design and the specific methods used for data collection (Kirkhart, 1995). A key consideration here is the extent to which the design components (Maxwell, 2013) are relevant to participants' lived experiences. Based on Kirkhart's (1995) framework to assess methodological validity, some questions you might pose might include, *Is the design informed by participants' cultural context(s)? Does the design include questions related to participants' interests, values, or concerns?*

Methodological validity also concerns assessments of your focus group protocol. Assessing your focus group protocol requires seeking feedback before the study begins and often results in revisions. If revisions to your protocol are made, you will want to record those changes. Doing so is useful to keep track of how your protocol has evolved. Furthermore, obtaining feedback strengthens your focus group protocol, by not only assessing its cultural appropriateness but also by making sure the focus group questions are relevant to the topic of interest and coherent. One method to obtain feedback is having a cultural guide or member of the community you plan to engage review the protocol. A trusted colleague, content expert or research/ evaluation team member are also candidates for reviewing the focus group protocol. The main goal of the review is to have reviewers put themselves in the position of the focus group participants, imagining how they might respond to the protocol (Maxwell, 2013).

Based on my review of the literature (AEA, 2011; Harding, 1991; Patton, 2015; Rodriguez, Schwartz, Lahman, & Geist, 2011; Yarbrough, Shulha, Hopson & Caruthers, 2011), my experience teaching qualitative methods for over a decade, and also in conducting focus groups, I developed a protocol feedback form (see Table 4.1 *Protocol Feedback Form*), including some central aspects of the culturally responsive stance advanced in this book as well as the fundamental aspects of qualitative interviews (as discussed in Chapter 3). After the reviewer has sufficient time to closely examine your focus group protocol, you will want to inquire about each aspect included in the protocol feedback form, soliciting specific recommendations for how the protocol can be improved.

Another way to attend to the cultural appropriateness of your focus group protocol is to conduct a pilot focus group. *Piloting* your focus group protocol requires locating and conducting a focus group with persons who have the same or similar characteristics as your potential participants. The purpose of this method is to generate feedback based on the experience of conducting an initial or "practice" focus group. However, piloting a focus group protocol may be challenging if the population of participants is limited, vulnerable, or hard-to-reach. In those cases, having a person review the protocol and provide feedback, as discussed above, becomes especially critical.

Methodological validity could also include checking your assumptions as an inquirer in terms of the participant's ability to answer the questions posed in the focus group protocol. This means it is necessary to be sensitive to whether participants, for example, have the requisite knowledge necessary to provide a thoughtful answer (Krueger & Casey, 2015). For instance, participants may not be able to answer a question if they have not had the experiences necessary to respond—one example being if the participant's

Table 4.1: *Protocol Feedback Form*

Aspect	Comments
Builds rapport (i.e., provides an opportunity for participants to describe who they are and how they wish to be identified, warm-up activity)	
Questions engage participants' culture from a strength-based perspective rather than a deficit perspective	
Questions use participants' terms and language where relevant	
Creates a space for participants' concerns/storytelling/meaningful interactions	
Includes open-ended questions	
Includes clear and coherent questions	
Uses probes and appropriate follow-up questions to elaborate meanings	
Interview questions cover a number of kinds of perceptions (i.e., experience, behavior, feeling, opinion questions)	
Demonstrates logical sequence of questions	
Uses guiding topics and transition sentences	
Closes with a show of appreciation for participants' insights and invites them to share anything they would like to add	

position within an organization does not involve the responsibilities or roles addressed in the question. Last, because the qualitative research community considers the researcher herself a data collection instrument (as discussed in Chapter 3), the inquirer needs to develop strong interpersonal competencies to maximize methodological validity (Symonette, 2004). The critical nature of the inquirer's interpersonal competencies for focus group validity is explicitly expressed in the third dimension of the multicultural validity framework: interpersonal validity.

Interpersonal Validity. This dimension speaks to the "soundness or trustworthiness of understanding emanating from personal interactions" (Kirkhart, 1995, p. 4). To address interpersonal validity, moderators continuously assess the extent to which their communications and behaviors toward focus group participants are culturally appropriate. Symonette (2004) elaborates on this point when she persuasively argues:

> Cultivating self-as-instrument and developing intercultural and multicultural competencies is a lifelong process and not a fixed state of being. Because culture is dynamic and ever-changing, yesterday's culturally competent practitioner could become tomorrow's incompetent. (p. 99)

In short, interpersonal validity demands that researchers engage in inquirer reflexivity, a topic that we will turn to later in the discussion.

Consequential Validity. This dimension centers on "the worth, adequacy, or appropriateness of actions resulting from the [research or] evaluation" (Kirkhart, 1995, p. 6). As discussed in Chapter 3, as agents for change, culturally responsive inquirers will use focus groups as vehicles for "empowerment, emancipation, or transformative learning" (Kirkhart, 2010, p. 4). At the least, culturally responsive inquirers intend no harm to participants. However, even the most well-intended culturally responsive focus group can have unintended negative outcomes. Here, I will stop to include Symonette's (2004) words as they hit the point of consequential validity squarely on the nose. She states, "what ultimately matters is not personal *intent* [emphasis in original] but rather an interpersonal *impact* [emphasis in original]" (p. 98). Consequential validity, then, is akin to Maxwell's (2013) notion of inquiry designs having consequences for people's lives. Both Maxwell (2013) and Kirkhart (2010) promote critical assessments of how the inquiry itself (overall design, focus groups) or the results from the inquiry impacted the lives of participants in both positive (social justice initiative), and negative ways. Questions to consider such assessments might include, *How will the findings from the inquiry be used? In what ways might the participants benefit from the data generated by these focus group questions? And, what are any potential consequences of the focus group findings for participants?*

The individual multicultural validity dimensions are interdependent, and work to establish the quality of culturally responsive focus groups when in interaction with each other. Inquirers who attend to the integration of validity dimensions will be better able to access, theorize, interpret, engage, and portray diverse points of view in meaningful and agentive ways.

I now return to a topic that was referred to in the discussion on interpersonal validity, that being inquirer reflexivity. Reflexivity was briefly mentioned in Chapter 2. In this section, I discuss how you can be more reflexive, deepening the understandings you have about yourself and others.

Inquirer Reflexivity

Inquirer reflexivity is advantageous because it better positions you to traverse the ever-changing landscape of cultural complexities, power differentials, social interactions, communication challenges, and ethical dilemmas you will encounter as a research instrument and agent for change. As defined in Chapter 2, inquirer reflexivity involves continuous assessments of your design, including the focus groups, and then adjustments to improve the research process (Lahman, Geist, Rodriguez, Graglia, & DeRoche, 2011; Maxwell, 2013). As evidenced by its definition, inquirer reflexivity is meant to improve the quality and character of the research process. There are three common mechanisms inquirers use to cultivate researcher reflexivity and enhance the quality of culturally responsive focus groups. These include reflective journaling, member checking, and triangulation.

Reflective Journaling. In research, *reflective journaling* involves creating a personal record of what one experiences as part of the inquiry process. Boud (2001) points out that the journal has two functions. It serves as "both the place where the events and experiences are recorded and the forum by which they are processed and re-formed" (p. 11). The forum researchers use to process and reexamine the experiences they have during the inquiry process can vary from diaries, to notebooks, to Word documents. Furthermore, reflective journaling is not limited to writing. Alternative forms such as art, poetry and other devices can be used to make meaning of, document, and reflect on feelings, thoughts, questions, and actions taken (Boud, 2001). Whether the reflection takes place before, during or after the focus group, reflective journaling is a powerful tool that enables the culturally responsive inquirer to dialogue with herself and process participants' cultural context (Janesick, 1999). In her discussion on journal writing, Janesick (1999) identifies multiple purposes for and benefits of reflective journal writing:

- Explore researcher subjectivities or cultural worldviews, histories, identities, experiences, values, assumptions, biases and how they might impact the focus group.

- Project the ethical issues and dilemmas that may be encountered during the focus group research process and problem solve how such challenges could be handled.

- Track changes in researcher thoughts, beliefs, behaviors, and interpretations.

- Illuminate the researcher role.

- Assess the researcher as a data collection instrument.

- Clarify understandings of participants' responses and concerns.

Some scholars recommend that reflective journal writing include others (Lahman et al., 2011). Creating spaces for dialogue with members of the focus group participants' community, colleagues or peers as part of the reflective journal process, for example, is especially valuable to challenge what you think you know and inquire about the cultural responsiveness of your focus group design, implementation, and results. Boud (2001) affirms the value of collective journal writing when he asserts: "It is only through a give and take with others and by confronting the challenges they pose that critical reflection can be promoted" (p. 15). Also, culturally responsive inquirers can invite focus group participants to dialogue with them about the inquiry. When used in this way, the journal serves as an "interactive tool" for communication (Janesick, 1999, p. 506). If focus group participants are invited to record their thoughts in a separate journal, reflective journaling offers a way to triangulate the researcher's thinking with the thinking of focus group participants (Janesick, 1999). Communications between the culturally responsive inquirer and focus group participants can also serve a member checking function. A topic that will be discussed in fuller detail later.

As mentioned at the top of this discussion, reflective journaling can occur at different focus group research stages: before, during and after. Inspired by the questions Boud (2001) proposed, below are some questions inquirers can pose to themselves or in collaboration with others to stimulate critical reflection on the different stages of research thereby strengthening the quality of their culturally responsive focus groups.

Before:

- How do people in the cultural context view things? What are the implications for me and the focus group design?

- What might I need to study or rehearse before I begin the focus group?

- How strongly do I hold my intents, and will these blind me to other possibilities of which I am yet unaware?

- What will I do if my assumptions about the focus group design are wrong?

- What will I be able to fall back on to cope effectively if the focus group does not go as planned?

During:

- What do I notice at this moment?

- What is happening in me at this moment? Around me?

- What is happening to others in this moment?

- How am I deciding to intervene (take action), or not, at this time?

- What decisions are being made by participants at this time?

After:

- Where does my interpretation of the experience lead me?

- What if I tried X?

Overall, reflective journaling contributes to the quality of culturally responsive focus groups as documenting and critiquing your thoughts, assumptions, feelings, and decisions exposes who you are as a culturally responsive knower and how you are perceived by others as culturally responsive inquirer (Symonette, 2004).

Member Checking. This technique involves "returning an interview or analyzed data to a participant" (Birt, Scott, Cavers, Campbell & Walter, 2016, p. 1802). Member checking aligns with cultural responsiveness because it reflects the meanings and voices of focus group participants and reduces the chance the researcher's voice will overpower focus group participants' interpretations. Reducing or decentering the researcher's voice also has the potential to limit researcher bias, which is one reason member checking is commonly relied upon to increase the quality of qualitative research, and focus groups in particular.

There is more than one way to member check. One method is to send the focus group transcript to participants, which can happen as soon as the transcriptions are complete. This approach will enable focus group participants to "check" the exactness of transcripts but not the credibility of the interpretations produced from the researcher's analysis of the focus group data (Birt et al., 2016). A second method is to use focus groups themselves for member checking. For example, investigators may decide to convene a focus group having participants review and discuss transcripts or interpretations. During a member check focus group, participants have opportunities to further co-construct and shift interpretations via modifying and or including information, not in the original data set (Birt et al., 2016). Focus group member checking is a more interactive approach given that participants can actively work as a group, co-constructing, and refining interpretations. Because analysis usually takes longer than transcription, sharing interpretations during a focus group is likely to happen weeks or months post data collection (Birt et al., 2016). A third method is to share preliminary interpretations with focus group participants. This approach is particularly empowering for focus group participants as it allows them to assess the extent to which they see their experiences reflected in the focus group findings. Moreover, having focus group participants review the analyzed focus group data can help ensure a fuller range of perspectives (i.e., dissenting, conflicting, or nonconforming, unpopular views) are represented, thereby enabling more robust interpretations. Yet, to fully capitalize on the advantages of this approach to member checking, analyzed data need to be submitted to participants in ways they can easily understand (Birt et al., 2016). For example, a member check document might include a summary of key findings or themes with quotes illustrating each one. For more detailed descriptions of member checking techniques, purposes, and documents see Birt et al. (2016). Finally, while presenting findings to focus group participants allows them to "check" researcher interpretations, this type of member checking is likely to occur well after the focus group has been conducted.

Triangulation. In his book, *The Research Act: A Theoretical Introduction to Sociological Methods*, Denzin (1973) proposes four types of triangulation. The first, *data triangulation*, might include conducting focus groups with different categories of people using the same protocol to compare results. This approach was used during an evaluation our team conducted in which focus group data from different persons (parents and teachers) were analyzed and compared. The second type, *investigator triangulation*, typically involves using more than one investigator to analyze the data. The analyzed data from each investigator would then be compared. Undergirding this type of triangulation is the assumption that similar findings from independent analyses of focus group data increase the credibility of results. Discrepancies in investigator findings can be resolved by additional data collection, further analysis, discussions, or a review of relevant literature. Of the different types of triangulation, *theoretical triangulation* is the least common. If this approach is used, it is important to assess the cultural congruence of the theories that will be used *before* collecting the focus group data as suggested by Kirkhart (2010). This will ensure the analysis appropriate for each theory can be used after the focus group data have been collected.

To conclude the chapter, I offer three points made by Birt et al. (2016) that I view important for culturally responsive inquirers to consider. First, people invited (focus group participants, other stakeholders, members of the community, etc.) to engage in assessments of quality (i.e., piloting, member checking) may ignore or decline invitations to participate. Being culturally responsive inquirers means accepting this fact. Second, when people accept invitations to participate in quality-enhancing endeavors, culturally responsive inquirers must make sure that the techniques used to enhance quality do not cause stress or place a significant burden on them. And third, inquirers need to not only establish the quality of their culturally responsive focus groups but also report all techniques used to bolster the quality of their focus group design.

Summary

In this chapter, I discussed how Kirkhart's (1995, 2010) multicultural validity framework and inquirer reflexivity can establish the quality of culturally responsive focus groups. Three additional mechanisms were recommended (reflective journaling, member checking, and triangulation) to support inquirer reflexivity. The case example displayed in Box 4.1 *Participant Expectations and Experiences of Engagement in an Online eLearning Nutrition Education Program*, reports how inquirer reflexivity was engaged to establish the quality of culturally responsive focus groups for an evaluation designed to assess an online eLearning nutrition education program for adults who have low incomes. The case example also highlights how some data analysis and interpretation techniques (discussed in Chapter 8) were applied to the focus group data. The following chapters continue to explore how culturally responsive focus groups have been applied in various disciplines with a range of marginalized groups.

Box 4.1 *Participant Expectations and Experiences of Engagement in an Online eLearning Nutrition Education Program*

Participant Expectations and Experiences of Engagement in an Online eLearning Nutrition Education Program

By Sarah Stotz, Ph.D. and Jung Sun Lee, Ph.D.

The purpose of this project was to develop and evaluate Food eTalk, an online eLearning nutrition education program designed to meet the needs of low-income adults in Georgia. This project included a multi-disciplinary team of faculty, staff, and students from the University of Georgia (UGA) Department of Food and Nutrition Supplemental Nutrition Assistance Program – Education (UGA SNAP-Ed), Cooperative Extension (CE), and College of Education. The primary researcher was a PhD student and registered dietitian. Focus groups were held at community-based venues including: HeadStart child care facilities, public libraries, CE offices, subsidized housing facilities, adult job-training facilities, and safety-net clinics.

A constructivist epistemology framed this study and supported a culturally responsive approach, in that it sees participants' perspectives as opportunities for co-creating knowledge rather than understanding one sole "Truth." Constructivism is built on the premise of social construction of reality, and one of the advantages of this approach is close collaboration between the researcher and the participant while enabling the participant to tell about his/her experiences. It is through this discourse that participants describe their views of reality which enables the researcher to better understand the participants' actions.

A case-study design framed this project with the Food eTalk program as the case. The focus group data used for the case study provided rich data regarding participants' experiences and perceptions of the program, augmenting the quantitative descriptive and pre/post knowledge or behavior data.

Focus group participants (n=45) were predominately female (96.8%), non-Hispanic African American (54.6%), living with children ≤18 years old (76.5%), and SNAP (formerly known as food stamps) recipients (62.5%). All participants were eligible for SNAP-Ed defined as living in households with income < 185% of the federal poverty level or other means-tested inclusion criterion.

The purpose of the focus groups was to understand participants' expectations (before using Food eTalk) and experiences (after using Food eTalk). Participants' stories about their experiences with Food eTalk helped the researcher understand how online nutrition education may (or may not) serve a wider audiences of low-income families in Georgia, and how to improve the program based on these experiences. Food eTalk, a culturally-tailored approach to nutrition education for low-income Georgians, featured a Southern-focused images, voices, actors and foods in eLearning activities and cooking videos. Each participant engaged in 2 focus groups, for a total of 16 focus groups (range 5-11 participants). Focus groups were ~75 minutes long and separated by 3 weeks (before and after using Food eTalk program).

Data were analyzed using a note-based constant comparison method including field notes, reflexivity memos, and transcriptions. A combination of inductive and deductive coding approaches was employed. The constant comparison approach included coding data, categorizing the codes, and reorganization of the categories into thematic representation through a series of assertions and interpretations. Using this method, data were compared across transcriptions to find similarities and differences, recognizing too, the researcher's own observations, ideas, and intuitions influenced this process. Analyses were facilitated by Atlas.ti.

Establishing quality and rigor is especially important area in scientific fields where quantitative inquiry is dominant. As aligned with culturally responsive focus group approach, the primary researcher kept a research journal to chronicle her own biases, positionality, investment in the direction of the focus group discussions. It was important to reflect on the journal, reflexivity memos, and a researcher subjectivity statement iteratively through data collection and analysis.

Major findings indicate these participants have ample smartphone-based Internet access and high self-efficacy using the Internet. They voiced desire for nutrition education with focus on disease-specific nutrition education, feeding 'picky' children, and recipes highlighting Southern cuisine. A key barrier to engagement in Food eTalk may be low motivation to use such a program. Inclusion of videos, interactive features, relevant content, and extrinsic incentives are important to increase motivation for user engagement. This research serves the UGA SNAP-Ed team as a foundation for evidence-based eLearning nutrition education program development for low-income audiences. Findings have been published in public health, nutrition, and community-based education journals and have been presented widely at local, national, and international conferences.

Several culturally-responsive strategies were employed to facilitate the focus groups with low-income adults, primarily focusing on creating a comfortable, respectful, and safe space for the participants to share their stories. First, focus groups were organized by a trusted educator or community member collaborator – as a means to gain entrée. Second, focus groups were held in spaces already familiar to participants to help them feel comfortable and confident in the physical space. Third, children were welcome at the focus groups as it was important to include the mothers' voices to understand how caregiving may impact eLearning experience, and many of our participants experienced challenges with accessing affordable childcare. Fourth, participants were compensated with gift cards. We believe this gesture was well received to show our respect for participants' volunteered time and resources. Fifth, the moderator reminded participants they are the "experts" on these topics, and that she was eager to learn from their unique experiences. Finally, participants who were late were welcomed into the focus group – as a means to accommodate some participant's challenges with transportation and other competing demands.

Lessons Learned

1) Several strategies may have enhanced cultural responsiveness of the focus groups. For example, given the focus group topics were primarily about nutrition, there are many easy food-focused "ice-breaker" activities that could have been quickly woven into the focus groups in hopes of enhancing participation during the interviews and providing space for organic conversation amongst the participants.

2) Had funding allowed, we would have provided a meal for focus group participants as an additional gesture of gratitude and a means to generate conversation.

3) It would have been helpful to better accommodate late arrivers as these individuals typically contributed less to focus group discussions than those who had been present during the introduction.

4) It is unclear the extent to which the Southern-focused images, voices, actors featured in Food eTalk impacted the participants' eLearning experiences. However, participants did note they appreciated the featured Southern foods as they were available (and affordable) in their local grocery.

Given most focus group participants were mothers of young children and all participants had limited/low income, it was ethically important to recognize that engagement (or not) in Food eTalk may or may not have been related to the program itself. Participants may have had stressful competing interests. Further, many of these participants may not have had experience participating in focus groups where their voices were valued and may not have been comfortable sharing details of their lives that impacted their experience. Based on these lessons learned, some recommendations include gathering in a physical space already familiar to participants, providing incentives as a gesture of gratitude and respect, providing a meal, adding an ice breaker at the start of the focus group to encourage participation and to accommodate participants who arrive late, and poignant, clear explanation that the participants' stories and experiences are what make them the experts on this "focused" topic.

Discussion Question

1. Researchers who desire to employ culturally responsive focus group methodology have the challenge of balancing time, respect for participants' stories, and, in the case of funded research, the agenda of the funder. These were all true of this particular project. How might the researcher plan to accommodate these various goals and stipulations?

References

American Evaluation Association (2011). *Public statement on cultural competence in evaluation.* Retrieved from https://www.eval.org/p/cm/ld/fid=92

Birt, L., Scott, S., Cavers, D., Campbell, C., & Walter, F. (2016). Member checking: A tool to enhance trustworthiness or merely a nod to validation? *Qualitative Health Research, 26*(13), 1802–1811.

Boud, D. (2001). Using journal writing to enhance reflective practice. *New Directions for Adult and Continuing Education, 2001*(90), 9–18.

Cypress, B. (2017). Rigor or reliability and validity in qualitative research: Perspectives, strategies, reconceptualization, and recommendations. *Dimensions of Critical Care Nursing, 36*(4), 253–263.

Denzin, Norman K. (1973). *The research act: A theoretical introduction to sociological methods.* New Jersey: Transaction Publishers.

Freeman, M., DeMarrais, K., Preissle, J., Roulston, K., & St. Pierre, E. A. (2007). Standards of evidence in qualitative research: An incitement to discourse. *Educational Researcher, 36*(1), 25–32.

Frierson, H., Hood, S., Hughes, G. & Thomas, V. (2010). A Guide to Conducting Culturally Responsive Evaluation. In National Science Foundation. *The 2010 User-Friendly Handbook for Project Evaluation.* National Science Foundation, Directorate for Education and Human Resources, Division of Research, Evaluation, and Communication. REC 99-12175 pp. 75–96.

Harding, S. (1991). *Whose science? whose knowledge? thinking from women's lives.* Ithaca, NY: Cornell University Press.

Janesick, V. J. (1999). A journal about journal writing as a qualitative research technique: History, issues, and reflections. *Qualitative Inquiry, 5*(4), 505–524.

Kirkhart, K. E. (1995). Seeking multicultural validity: A postcard from the road. *Evaluation Practice, 16*, 1–12.

Kirkhart, K. E. (2005). Through a cultural lens: Reflections on validity and theory in evaluation. In S. Hood, R. Hopson, & H. Frierson (Eds.), *The role of culture and cultural context: A mandate for inclusion, the discovery of truth, and understanding in evaluative theory and practice* (pp. 21–39). Greenwich, CT: Information Age Publishing.

Kirkhart, K. E. (2010). Eyes on the prize: Multicultural validity and evaluation theory. *American Journal of Evaluation, 31*(3), 400–413.

Krueger, R. A. & Casey, M. A. (2015). *Focus groups: A practical guide for applied research* (5th ed.). Thousand Oaks, CA: Sage.

Lahman, M., Geist, M., Rodriguez, K., Graglia, P., & DeRoche, K. (2011). Culturally responsive relational reflexive ethics in research: The three rs. *Quality and Quantity: International Journal of Methodology, 45*, 1397–1414.

Lavallée, L. F. (2009). Practical application of an Indigenous research framework and two qualitative Indigenous research methods: Sharing circles and Anishnaabe symbol-based reflection. *International Journal of Qualitative Methods, 8*(1), 21–40.

Lincoln, Y. S., & Guba, E. G. (1985). Establishing trustworthiness. *Naturalistic Inquiry, 289*, 331.

Maxwell, J. A. (2013). *Research design: An interactive approach.* Thousand, Oaks, CA: Sage.

Patton, M. Q. (2015). *Qualitative evaluation and research methods.* Thousand Oaks, CA: Sage.

Rodriguez, K., Schwartz, J., Lahman, M., & Geist, M. (2011). Culturally responsive focus groups: Reframing the research experience to focus on participants. *The International Journal of Qualitative Methods, 10*(4), 400–417.

Spiers, J., Morse, J. M., Olson, K., Mayan, M., & Barrett, M. (2018). Reflection/commentary on a past article: "Verification strategies for establishing reliability and validity in qualitative research." *International Journal of Qualitative Methods, 17*, 1–2.

Symonette, H. (2004). Walking pathways towards becoming a culturally competent evaluator: Boundaries, borderlands and border-crossings. In M. Thompson-Robinson, R. Hopson, & S. SenGupta (Eds.), *In search of cultural competence in evaluation: Toward principles and practices [Special issue]. New Directions for Evaluation,* (pp. 95–109). San Francisco, CA: Jossey-Bass.

Tracy, S. J. (2010). Qualitative quality: Eight "big-tent" criteria for excellent qualitative research. *Qualitative Inquiry, 16*(10), 837–851.

Yarbrough, D. B., Shulha, L. M., Hopson, R. K., & Caruthers, F. A. (2011). *The program evaluation standards: A guide for Evaluators and Evaluation Users* (3rd ed.). Thousand Oaks, CA: Sage.

CHAPTER FIVE

Culturally Responsive Focus Groups with Youths and Older Adults

In This Chapter

TRADITIONALLY, INQUIRY HAS EITHER ignored youths (children and adolescents) and older adults (over the age of 65) or worked with them from a deficit-orientation. In this chapter, I discuss how inquirers are increasingly recognizing the valuable contributions young people and the elderly can make to scientific knowledge and how inquiry with these groups is being conducted from more of a strength-based orientation. Specifically, I attend to how focus groups have been used with young people and older adults to gather information on a wide range of topics in culturally sensitive ways. I also discuss issues particular to these groups (i.e., peer pressure, health conditions), special focus group strategies including how to increase focus group participation, and special ethical concerns. In addition, I present two case examples to demonstrate many of the points made in the chapter. The first, *"I don't understand the question?": Focus Groups with Transnational Migrant Newcomer Youths in Evaluation*, discusses gathering focus group data from migrant newcomer youths in a library-based program drawing on an asset-based approach. The second case example, *Photo Elicitation Focus Groups with Older Adults*, provides insights on how different types of photographs were used during focus groups to elicit information from participants over the age of 65 for an evaluation of a healthy aging program.

Culturally Responsive Focus Groups with Youths

Traditional social science approaches conduct research *on* youths (Oakley, 1994). These approaches are heavily influenced by the perspective that positions minors as incomplete adults (Danby & Farrell, 2004). In contrast, recent sociological perspectives encourage research *with* or *for* youngsters (Danby & Farrell, 2004; Oakley, 1994) and suggest that minors are persons complete with values, viewpoints and agency (Greene & Hogan, 2005). The culturally responsive stance articulated in this book aligns with this recent thinking on conducting research with youths. Positioning minors as persons infers that they can construct knowledge and are the experts of their experience (Borkhorst-Heng & Keating Marshall, 2019). However, understandings of *who* is a youth varies depending on the culture. In the United States, for example, youth can include the period of childhood (from approximately 6 to 10 years of age) and adolescence (from approximately 11 to 18 years of age).

Researchers increasingly acknowledge the ability of young people of various ages and from different grade levels to describe and interpret their choices, activities, environments, processes, and everyday routines. For instance, researchers have conducted focus groups with participants ages 11 to 14 to gain their viewpoint on topics such as health and illness (Horner, 2000) and participants from grades 5 to 8 to explore cyberbullying (Mishna, Saini, & Solomon, 2009). Researchers deem focus groups appropriate for gathering information from minors because they promote interaction and encourage conversation among peers (Hoppe, Wells, Morrison, Gillmore, & Wilsdon, 1995). Focus groups may make youths feel comfortable, because they mimic the small group classroom settings "where conversation seems to flow effortlessly" (Mauthner, 1997, p. 23). In addition, focus groups tend to shift the power imbalance between the adult moderator and minor participants by virtue of the fact there are more youngsters than adults (Horner, 2000).

While focus groups create possibilities for youths to share more information about themselves, there are some aspects of youth culture and focus group design that can create barriers to stimulating discussion and interaction. Because of this, reflexive vigilance on the part of the culturally responsive inquirer is necessary to monitor how young people are responding to the focus group design and make changes accordingly. Below, I discuss some aspects to be mindful of when developing and implementing culturally responsive focus groups with youths.

Peer Pressure. Within the context of a focus group, peer pressure has both negative and positive consequences (Horner, 2000). On the one hand, peer pressure can create a situation where children and adolescents decide not to share their perspective, seeking to conform to the opinions of those in the group. Horner (2000) notes that in cases like this, the focus group data are then restricted as contrasting perspectives are not captured. On the other hand, peer pressure can increase data quality as participants disclose more information in an effort to be like others in the group who are freely expressing their experiences (Horner, 2000). For this reason, it is important to establish an atmosphere where young people feel comfortable sharing opposing or contrasting perspectives (Horner, 2000). This can be accomplished by emphasizing ground rules that all participants should be respectful of others and that all opinions, including contrasting viewpoints, are valued. Additionally, careful attention must be paid to how young people are interacting and reacting to each other's comments throughout the focus group. If, for example, a particular youth dominates the conversation, that person may be thanked for her contribution but then reminded that the input of others is valued as well, offering an opportunity for the other youth to speak.

Sensitive Topics and Group Composition. When discussing potentially sensitive or stigmatizing situations, participating in a focus group is generally a valuable experience for children and adolescents as they can receive support from other peers in the group (Morgan, 2019). Nevertheless, the comfort level of youths needs to be closely attended to while discussing sensitive topics (Hoppe et al., 1995). Referencing Greenbaum (1990) and Basch (1987), Hoppe et al., (1995) offer a strategy to reduce the anxiety level of minors when discussing sensitive topics; they suggest "warming up to sensitive topics with introductions, general comments (e.g., remarks about current events), and nonthreatening questions, introducing the more sensitive ones once the group seems at ease" (p.110).

Researchers recommend youth focus groups be homogenous, particularly concerning gender when discussing sensitive topics (Hoppe et al., 1995, p.106). However, a mixed-gender focus group can work with younger children and less sensitive topics (Mishna et al., 2000). For example, when Davis and Jones (1996) used mixed-gender focus groups to explore how primary school children (9-11 years old) and secondary school children (13-14 years old) navigate their local environment, they reported how the mixed-gender composition worked well for primary school children but less well for the secondary school children. They state:

> In our study the mixed focus group approach worked well with 9-11-year olds but had to be adapted for the 13-14-year olds, where the agendas of teenage girls and boys turned out to be not only quite different but conflicting and had a negative impact on group discussion. The forming of eight single-sex groups in the secondary schools resulted in the gathering of some of the richest material in the study. (Davis & Jones, 1996, p. 366)

Therefore, whether a mixed- or same-gender focus group is used will depend on the sensitivity of the topic and age of the youths.

Sample Size and Segmentation. Smaller groups (ranging from 4 to 5 participants) are ideal for helping to maintain the attention of young participants in focus groups (Hoppe et al., 1995; Morgan, Gibbs, Maxwell, & Britten, 2002). In addition to the reduction of focus group size, segmentation is sometimes necessary when developing youth focus groups (Morgan, 2019) to avoid large discrepancies in age between focus group participants (Charlesworth 1997; Gibson 2007) as the presence of older children may negatively impact the participation of younger children (Hoppe et al., 1995).

An evaluation conducted by Levine and Zimmerman (1996) exemplifies a focus group design that included segmentation. The evaluation examined the effectiveness of a media communications campaign designed to reduce youth violence and included nine focus groups with 73 ethnically diverse participants (predominately African American and Latinx, several Asian and White) aged 8-24. All participants were at risk for violence. In this case, the researchers were using segmentation to not only respond to the wide range in participants' ages but also their different experiences and gender.

For instance, of the nine focus groups, two focus groups were conducted with young persons aged 8-12 (one male and one female group), one focus group was conducted with boys aged 12-19, one focus group was conducted with girls aged 17-19, four focus groups were conducted with young adults aged 18-24 (two female and two male groups), and one was a mixed group conducted with young adults aged 18-24. Levine and Zimmerman (1996) state that the separate focus groups with younger children were appropriate because "it seemed likely that youths aged 18 and younger (who were still likely to be in the educational system) would have different attitudes toward the messages and materials than older youths" (p. 367). The researchers also state that segmentation, including a separate mixed group with participants aged 18-24 was purposeful to understand experiences of the media campaign from the perspective of those who were both homeless and victims of violence.

Focus Group Participation. To encourage active participation among young people, I recommend focusing exercises. As discussed in Chapter 3, focusing exercises use stimuli (i.e., text, photos, drawings) to encourage discussion among participants on a topic (Bloor, Frankland, Thomas, & Stewart, 2001). Focusing exercises are advised when working with children and adolescents, because they stimulate thinking and interaction without making the moderator the center of attention, as well as allow youths with different abilities and skills to share their experiences. For example, mapping exercises and photovoice were used by Darbyshire et al. (2005) to gain insights from children aged between 4 and 12 years to discuss and depict their views on physical activity or play related to their environment. Darbyshire et al. (2005) assert using these focusing exercises honored the children's agency as well as their ability to (verbally and nonverbally) express and interpret their viewpoints.

Moderating Focus Groups. Another key consideration is how young people might respond to the questions and activities posed. For instance, if focus groups with youths are held in school contexts, participants may respond to moderators as they would to adults in the classroom (i.e., raising their hands and only speaking when directly asked a question) (Darbyshire et al., 2005). Whereas these communication norms have their place in classroom settings, they can work against the intended interactive and spontaneous nature of the focus group format and negatively impact the quality of the data. Moderators, then, need to be mindful of how participants are responding to their questions and any stimuli provided, and make adjustments accordingly. For instance, after noticing how youths were following school communication norms rather than actively engaging in a discussion, the "facilitator changed the environment by asking everyone if they would like to jump and talk, signaling a more fun and interactive norm of communication (Darbyshire et al., 2005, p. 422). In addition, to engage young people in focus groups and promote an atmosphere of equity, or decrease the adult-child hierarchy, moderators can conduct focus groups in more informal environments (i.e., community centers), encourage youths to call them by their first names, and modify seating arrangements or their seating position (i.e., moderator sits on the floor) (Morgan et al., 2002, p. 9).

Recruitment and Incentives. Recruiting minors to participate in focus groups is particularly complex and challenging as parents or a legal guardian can deny permission for their child to participate in the study, even after the child has consented to participate (Danby & Farrell, 2004). For this reason, child and parent participation in focus group research is commonly incentivized. To illustrate this point, Morgan et al. (2002), report: "recognizing that children—like adults—have economic lives, we compensated children with a $5 gift voucher for their participation as well as offering expenses to parents" (p.8). In the Levine and Zimmerman (1996) media campaign evaluation mentioned earlier, each participant, except for those aged 8-12, received $20 reimbursement for travel and any miscellaneous expenses associated with the study. All participants, including the youngest groups, received a *Youth Against Violence: Choose to De-Fuse* poster, a baseball-type hat, a T-shirt, and a pin. (p. 367)

The Levin and Zimmerman (1996) evaluation makes clear that financial rewards may not be the most suitable for young children. Thanking children for their participation and offering feedback about the focus group study are often sufficient incentives (Gibson, 2007).

Ethical Considerations

A common rule instituted by ethical committees is to require that researchers secure consent from both the parent (legal guardian) and the minor. However, because youths require permission from a legal guardian to participate in research, it is perhaps more accurate to regard minors as giving assent rather than consent. Also, ethical practice demands that both minors and their legal guardians be fully informed about the purposes and procedures of the focus group. To ensure an informed consent process for both minors and their legal guardians, researchers have incorporated different strategies. Darbyshire et al. (2005), for instance, noted how the schools, parents, and youths were provided with "child-friendly" documents, which included all of the study details (p. 421). In another study, researchers provided each participant with a written consent form to sign (or make a mark on the paper instead of a signature) to indicate their consent (Danby & Farrell, 2004). The form and other information regarding the study were sent home to parents. The researchers also visited the classrooms and discussed the research process directly with the children, allowing the children to ask questions about the research (Danby & Farrell, 2004).

It should be noted that the consent process can also extend to how the youth focus group data can be used. In most cases, the consent process makes clear that what is said during the focus group will be used for research purposes. However, if focusing exercises are included as part of the focus group (i.e., drawings, mapping, photovoice), researchers will want to request permission to use the images and explain how the images will be used (Darbyshire et al., 2005).

Summary

Conducting culturally responsive focus groups with children and adolescents demands a willingness to decenter adults and respect the meanings that minors, as people, assign to their perspectives. Tapping into the world of young people requires diligence and creativity. As discussed in this chapter, inquirers have multiple strategies at their disposal to thoughtfully engage children and adolescents in focus groups. Notwithstanding, culturally responsive youth focus groups are only effective to the degree that the inquirer is attentive to the focus group dynamics, and can accommodate the diversity of youths' culture, including but not limited to their abilities, communication styles, and varied interests.

In the case example (see Box 5.1 *"I don't understand the question?"*: *Focus Groups with Transnational Migrant Newcomer Youth in Evaluation*), the evaluators describe how the application of an asset-based approach and multicultural validity (as discussed in Chapter 4) initiated changes to their focus groups with newcomer migrant youths, which in turn centered the linguistic diversity of the young people, positioning them as experts of their experiences. The case example also highlights how the focus groups fostered deeper understandings of culture and advanced social justice efforts relevant to the context.

Box 5.1 *"I don't understand the question?"*: *Focus Groups with Transnational Migrant Newcomer Youth in Evaluation*

"I don't understand the question?": Focus Groups with Transnational Migrant Newcomer Youths in Evaluation

by Sophia Rodriguez, PhD with Jeremy Acree

The setting is a public library in Hartford, CT,[1] which has a long history of serving the immigrant community. Our mixed methods evalu-

---

1 This program is funded through a grant from the Institute for Museum Library Services.

ation (2016-2019) investigates how a program at the public library, in partnership with a public school district, increases belonging for newcomer migrant youths (e.g., refugee, undocumented, displaced, and unaccompanied and are 0-30 months in the United States). The program sought to increase belonging for newcomers by drawing on the institutional support of the library as a democratic space. Specifically, the program curriculum focused on civic awareness of state and local policies impacting newcomers, how to access public and social resources in Hartford, and how to engage in activism in the community. The following questions guided the evaluation of the program: 1) How do newcomer migrant youths define belonging? 2) To what extent do newcomer youths in a library-based program experience belonging?

Our evaluation leveraged a critical perspective on the sociological concept of belonging (Rodriguez, in press) because studies of migrants are necessarily about their belonging (Malsbury, 2014). Previous literature narrowly associates belonging with English proficiency and assimilation (Gonzales, Suarez-Orozco, & Dedios-Sanguineti, 2013). Thus, this evaluation took an asset-based (Jaffe-Walter & Lee, 2018) approach to uncover the factors that enhance young migrant belonging through the library-based program.

The young participants varied in country of origin, age, languages spoken, but were recruited for this program due to their newcomer status (0-30 months in the United States). The kids in Cohort 1 (N=22) represent countries in Africa, Asia, and Latin/Central America, speaking languages such as Arabic, French, Karen, Spanish, and Swahili. Newcomers in Cohort 2 (N=14), are primarily from Puerto Rico, Peru, El Salvador, and Ecuador, and are Spanish speakers.

Our evaluation was in response to Boyce and Chouinard's (2017) call to move beyond the buzzword of "culturally responsive approaches" to evaluation to interrogate "culture" in meaningful, asset-based ways. Therefore, in this project, we examined how power operated in micro-ways (Foucault, 1982) through techniques such as English language use during data collection and how it was disrupted when the evaluator elected to adjust focus group protocols in the moment and leverage multiple languages, enabling the migrant youths to broker languages for each other and share in the process of knowledge production during the focus groups.

The evaluation approach we used, culturally responsive evaluation (CRE), centers culture during each stage of evaluation practice, from initial engagement with stakeholders to framing questions and ultimately analyzing and disseminating findings (Hood, Hopson, & Kirkhart, 2015). Additionally, CRE incorporates cultural awareness and sensitivity into arguments for the validity and quality of evaluative practice, building from Kirkhart's (1995) notion of "multicultural validity." Cultural responsiveness is also recognized as necessary when working with historically marginalized populations both within the United States and internationally, particularly when transformation and emancipation are established as the aspirations of the programs and policies being evaluated (Cram & Mertens, 2016). In theorizing culture, however, there remains what Chouinard (2014) refers to as "enduring issues of practice, defined as underlying areas of practice that generate perplexing questions requiring further consideration" (p. 342). This evaluation foregrounded this transfer of cultural responsiveness.

The focus groups gathered information from young migrant newcomers about how the library-based program was fostering their sense of belonging to school and community, and to triangulate data. The evaluator had a strong awareness of their cultural backgrounds and investigated them through ethnographic-oriented interviews, participant observations and fieldwork, reflecting upon emergent dilemmas related to language. The participants (N=36) were selected randomly. The focus groups were conducted approximately every 3 months with four-five youths and lasted between 60-90 minutes. The evaluator developed two separate focus group protocols that aligned with elements of the curriculum/program to collect data on the youths' ongoing sense of belonging and experiences in the library program.

The first focus group focused on questions related to demographics, migration journeys, and challenges adjusting to the United States. The second focus group asked more specific questions about school experiences and activities at the library. In the second focus group, a young person remarked, "I don't understand the question." This prompted the evaluator to reflect upon how this process of asking questions in English, in a culturally relevant approach, was invariably useless for some students given their newcomer status with limited English language facility.[2]

The findings demonstrated how the library-based program increases social belonging for newcomer migrant youths. Key to their increased sense of belonging was feeling a "sense of solidarity," to one another because they are all "in the same boat learning English" (Rodriguez, in press). The participants felt a connection because of their experiences as newcomers, and thus desired to share their migration journeys, family separation, and the political violence and civil unrest in their home countries such as Honduras, Liberia, and Honduras. These stories emerged during the focus groups through speaking in multiple languages and brokering meaning to the evaluator. From these findings, we were able to advocate for a social worker for the project due to what was gleaned during the focus groups. The findings were disseminated in bi-monthly reports to community partners and through collaborative academic publications (Rodriguez, 2019; Rodriguez, Naficy, & Russo (2020).

Lessons Learned

One of the lessons learned was related to what "culture" or "culturally relevant" means when conducting focus groups. In this evaluation, normal procedures—i.e., having a focus group protocol aligned with evaluation aims—were disrupted because participants did not always speak the same language. Thus, being "responsive" in this project meant adjusting roles and understanding children and young adults as experts in making meaning of their own experiences. In this sense, a culturally responsive approach does not offer a universal method for "understanding" culture, but requires ongoing flexibility and reflexivity in response to a given context. Language barriers prohibited a connection with newcomers, prompting evaluators to consider the colonization process at play with English dominance in schools and research spaces (Delevan, et al., 2017). This is not to say that evaluators/researchers must be multilingual. Rather, an important lesson for evaluators to keep in mind is to engage in reflection and critique about what it means to be culturally

---

2 We intentionally use facility as opposed to proficiency to counteract deficit-discourses about minoritized groups.

responsive in the process of collecting data if language is a barrier. Reyes (2019) notes that the "English-is-all-that-matters approach promotes a deficit discourse" blinding researchers instead of pausing to be disrupted.

Another lesson learned was the importance of engaging young migrants as "cultural brokers." A cultural broker is defined as "bridging, linking, mediating between groups to effect change" (Reyes, 2019, p. 532). This strategy is more than transmitting information. Rather, young people are mediating in ways that yield mutual understanding and meaning. This critical strategy relied upon an asset-based approach to migrant youths' belonging. In other words, "cultural brokering" as a form of communication during data collection served to "take action into the world" rather than allowing adults' perspectives to govern youth experiences (Orellana, 2009, p. 533). As evaluators consider conducting CRE approaches, being attentive to backgrounds, traumas, and language differences is necessary for demonstrating cultural responsiveness as we are held answerable/accountable to participants (Patel, 2016). Additionally, evaluators must be prepared to have their authority disrupted. By this, we mean evaluators need to consider translating or engaging in translanguaging practices so that youth can collaborate in the evaluation process.

A final lesson learned relates to the ethics of conducting focus groups with sensitive populations. These youths were refugees, undocumented, unaccompanied, and some had experienced interrupted schooling and trauma. As such, building relationships was critical, which challenges the content of the focus group. Many were initially reticent due to the technology and formal nature of the evaluation process, so ensuring the process is explained through the means of cultural brokering would have been a better strategy.

This case example shows how disrupting power relations—such as English dominance—in focus groups, and leveraging multiple languages and youths' cultural and linguistic brokering enhanced the focus group as a data source in this evaluation. Evaluators must risk being disrupted in their process. This allows for enhanced meaning-making with multilingual and multicultural populations. A question that remains is how to best prepare researchers and evaluators for these complex contexts that are attentive to deeper meanings of culture and ethics.

Discussion Questions

1. How might conventional methods and instruments (e.g., focus group protocols) conflict with or undermine culturally responsive aims?

2. In addition to language differences, what other aspects of research/ methodology may influence power relations between researchers and participants? How might evaluators respond in culturally responsive ways?

Culturally Responsive Focus Groups with Older Adults

Who constitutes an older adult depends on the project. Most gerontology researchers include individuals over 65 years of age in this category (Brondani, MacEntee, Bryant, & O'Neill, 2008; Krause, Chatters, Meltzer, & Morgan, 2000; Melenhorst, Rogers, & Bouwhuis, 2006). In consideration of this research, I also identify older adults as persons over 65 years of age. Further, it should be noted that research related to this age group has historically focused on their health, particularly their *presumed* declining physical ability (Reichstadt, Depp, Palinkas, Folsom, & Jeste, 2007). Attending to the health issues of the elderly is important, however, solely focusing on negative health challenges promotes a deficit orientation. Recently, gerontology research has turned its attention to resiliency among older adults as their level of functioning changes (Halpin et al., 2017; Halpin, 2018). An increased focus on resiliency reflects a more strength-based or culturally-sensitive orientation, recognizing the capacity of older adults to adjust, despite any life changes they may experience. In addition, researchers are capitalizing on the unique knowledge seniors have to offer. Increasingly researchers are eliciting the opinions of older adults on a range of topics via focus groups. For example, researchers have used focus groups to gather insights from older adults about their online learning experiences (Morrison, Lichtenwald, & Tang, 2019) and technology usage and attitudes (Mitzner et al., 2010).

The culturally responsive stance advanced in this book embraces the differences in how older adults age, treats their experiences and perceptions as a rich knowledge source, and attempts to understand and respond to the unique needs of this community (Cohen, Sandel, Thomas, & Barton, 2004). From this perspective, culturally responsive inquirers are charged with understanding the abilities and needs of the older adults they are working with and accommodating the focus group design accordingly. To assist with this charge, pertinent aspects of conducting culturally responsive focus groups with older adults are discussed in the sections below.

Accommodating Health Conditions and Maintaining Attention. Researchers must be sensitive to how a wide variety of health conditions may impact older adults' ability to attend or sustain engagement in focus groups (Barrett & Kirk, 2000). For instance, some elders may not be able to attend focus groups if they are managing many health-related appointments. To offset the contingencies that may limit older adults' ability to attend a focus group, it is recommended that researchers over-recruit numbers of participants (Barrett & Kirk, 2000). Geriatric participants may experience fatigue during the focus group session (Barrett & Kirk, 2000; Hawthorne et al., 2006).

To help avoid participant fatigue undermining the goals of the focus group, I offer two strategies. Researchers can shorten the duration of a focus group, or include a break. Bear in mind, however, that either of these strategies can limit the number of topics covered during the session (Barrett & Kirk, 2000). Some individuals have difficulties with sight and hearing. To help the flow in these situations, it is suggested that such individuals be seated close to other participants (Quine & Cameron, 1995 as cited in Bloor et al., 2001, p. 27), and to the moderator (Barrett & Kirk, 2000). Smaller focus group sessions with adapted visuals (i.e., flip charts, documents) may be helpful for individuals with impaired vision (Morgan, 2019). Furthermore, the lighting in the room should be sufficient for older adults to see materials without difficulty (Barrett & Kirk, 2000).

The interactive nature of a focus group can place high memory and attention demands on older adults. For example, Barrett & Kirk (2000) report that when a moderator returned to an older adult speaker who was initially interrupted by another member of the focus group, the interrupted speaker "forgot what they started to say, even when reminded of their first few words and the discussion leading up to their interrupted remark" (p. 626). In other cases, attention can be diverted from the research topic because older adults use the focus group as a "therapy session, taking the opportunity to speak about their particular problems rather than concentrating on the issues generated by the moderator" (Barrett & Kirk, 2000, p. 625).

Sensitive Topics. Older adults may be uncomfortable discussing private matters in a focus group setting. To stimulate discussion on difficult topics, focusing exercises are recommended. For example, to discuss the potentially sensitive topic of oral health and related health disorders with seniors, Brondani, MacEntee, Bryant, and O'Neill (2008) utilized vignettes or short, hypothetical stories. They claim the vignette "prompted a more elaborate discussion of issues around dental pain, toothlessness, and appearance, than what might otherwise have occurred without the prompt" (Brondani, MacEntee, Bryant, & O'Neill, 2008, p. 1150). Based on their focus group research, Brondani et al., (2008) assert vignettes are effective when discussing sensitive topics with elderly participants for three reasons. First, the story or scenario can be modified for use by participants from different cultural backgrounds. Second, participants can discuss a sensitive topic in response to the scenario provided, rather than disclose personal information to other people in the focus group. And third, vignettes create opportunities for enhanced interaction among the participants themselves.

Sample Size and Segmentation. Sample size is an important consideration when developing culturally responsive focus groups for older adults; however there is no consensus among researchers as to the ideal number of participants. Some studies have implemented small focus groups comprised of three to five participants (Adler & Rottunda, 2006). Others have used slightly larger groups, ranging in size from four to nine people in a group (Mitzner et al., 2010). Depending on the purposes of your investigation, you may determine it is best to separate participants by category (Morgan, 2019). A study on older adults' technology usage and attitudes provides an example of segmentation. For this study, Mitzner et al., (2010) divided participants into two categories: "low education" and "high education" (p. 1711). According to this study "seniors in the low education groups had less than a college degree (46% of participants), whereas those in the high education groups had obtained a college degree or higher (54% of participants)" (p. 1711). Researchers report that separating the seniors into these categories was purposeful to determine if there were any significant differences in technology experiences between the high and low education groups (Mitzner et al., 2010).

Focus Group Participation. If older people don't have adequate transportation or don't drive at night, it may be difficult for them to participate in a focus group meeting (Krause, 2002). Therefore, responsiveness may include scheduling focus groups during the day, conducting focus groups where participants regularly attend meetings (i.e., place of worship, clubhouse, community center, retirement home), or providing transportation for participants (Barrett & Kirk, 2000; Krause, 2002). To support the participation of their focus group members with mobility issues, Northridge et al., (2017) arranged for taxis to pick them up and bring them home. Establishing rapport within the focus group also aids participation. Strategies that build rapport with older adult participants include:

(a) allowing the participants to collectively select the best time for the meeting

(b) providing name tags to encourage the use of first names

(c) providing refreshments (Brondani, MacEntee, Bryant, & O'Neill, 2008, p. 1148)

Also, establishing an environment that supports older persons' participation in focus groups is vital. To do this, it is recommended that the focus group session is in a setting that has few, if any, stairs to climb. It should also have comfortable chairs and a hospitable room temperature (Barrett & Kirk, 2000). Moreover, the setting needs to have adequate space for mobility devices such as canes, wheelchairs, crutches, and walkers (Quine and Cameron, 1995 as cited in Bloor et al., 2001, p. 27).

Moderating Focus Groups. The moderator's facilitation skills play an important role when conducting focus groups with seniors. This skill set includes communicating clearly, listening carefully, allowing participants adequate time to think about the question, and encouraging them to elaborate on their responses (Barrett & Kirk, 2000). It is also a good idea to allow only one person to speak at a time. This eases the transcription process and also reduces the "difficulties that elderly people experience in dividing attention between more than one speaker" (Barrett & Kirk, 2000, p. 627). Also, researchers suggest that older adults may be more comfortable with a focus group facilitator who is close to their own age (Barrett & Kirk, 2000).

Recruitment and Incentives. In general, when recruiting elderly people, it is advised to place announcements where they are likely to congregate (i.e., community centers, retirement homes) and live (Brondani, MacEntee, Bryant & O'Neill, 2008). As an aid in recruitment, gerontology researchers have also enlisted the assistance of people in the community and focus group participants themselves (snowball sampling) (Reichstadt et al., 2007). It should be noted that the sampling pool of available older adults for focus group participation might be skewed toward female participants (Hawthorne et al., 2006). For example, in their cross cultural research investigating older adults' quality of life in countries such as Spain, Brazil, Hungary, Denmark, Japan, China, and Israel, Hawthorne et al., (2006) state that females were overrepresented in their focus groups "because they were easier to access, their greater life longevity and willingness to talk about QoL [quality of life] issues" (Hawthorne et al., 2006, p.1262). If female experiences are the focus of the investigation, this will not necessarily be an issue. However, if more gender balance is needed for the topic under investigation, it may be necessary to focus more energy on recruiting men.

Financial incentives are also used. In a study investigating older adults' motivations for adopting technology, American participants received $25 for their participation, and Dutch participants received €10 (Melenhorst et al., 2006). Nevertheless, money is not the only incentive for elderly participants. In their study, Barrett and Kirk (2000) used focus groups with elderly and disabled elderly persons in the United Kingdom to determine the support they need to live as independently as possible. These scholars report that elders who participated in their study were motivated by the opportunity to learn and also by the refreshments offered. Other researchers have noted how providing food was incentivizing and responsive to the needs of the senior focus group attendees "who often packed up the remaining food afterwards and brought it home" (Northridge et al., 2017, p. 8).

Ethical Considerations

The methodological literature offers some strategies to enhance the informed consent process with older adult focus group participants. Barrett and Kirk (2000) sent an invitation letter (in large print—14 pt. font) a couple of weeks before the focus group explaining the project. They then reviewed the project details just before the focus group meeting began. Based on their review of the literature on informed consent with elderly people, Sugarman, McCrory, and Hubal (1998) report using a nontraditional technique for obtaining informed consent; they show a video with the project information. These same scholars note that using alternative informed consent strategies when designing and conducting consent procedures was especially critical when obtaining informed consent from participants with less formal education.

The confidentiality of older adults is particularly worthy of attention as some have already experienced a loss of privacy and dignity as a result of living in a group setting or no longer being able to live independently. Concerns about privacy and confidentiality may also preclude some older adults from participating or continuing their participation in focus groups, particularly if the group consists largely of strangers. Thus, assuring elders that their participation is voluntary is crucial.

Summary

Inquirers have found focus groups suitable for gathering information from older adults on a wide range of topics and issues. In the context of culturally responsive focus groups, it is critical to implement focus groups in ways that appreciate the variability in the aging process; work against ageism; handle elderly adults and their concerns with care; and accommodate older adults' needs, including an informed consent process that is sensitive to their privacy and dignity. The following case example, Box 5.2 *Photo-Elicitation Focus Groups with Older Adults*, highlights how a culturally responsive evaluator conducted focus groups with adult participants over the age of 65 using a theoretical model that recognizes their capacity to respond to changes in their life. This researcher also utilized an alternative approach, photo-elicitation, to access and center their cultural insights. This case example also addresses challenges including obtaining informed consent, the use of technology, and shows how these issues were addressed.

Box 5.2 *Photo-Elicitation Focus Groups with Older Adults*

Photo-Elicitation Focus Groups with Older Adults
by Nuria Jaumot-Pascual, PhD

This project focused on the evaluation of a healthy aging program (HAP) for adults over the age of 65. The focus groups focused on participants' experiences in the program. The setting of this evaluation was an organization serving elderly adults in the U.S. Southeast. The HAP was a 6-month-long program that offered health promotion activities with 31 participants. Eight of them participated in photo elicitation focus groups. These participants were mostly Black (75%), female (75%), low to extremely low income (88%), and 73 years old on average. All eight participants had chronic conditions, four also had mobility impairments, and two had cognitive decline.

I situated myself as a Values-Engaged, Educative evaluator (Greene, DeStefano, Burgon, & Hall, 2006), which committed me to engage with critical values, engage in the evaluation as an educative process, and to learn how the program performed for participants. I used transformative parallel mixed methods designs (Mertens, 2014) that used photoelicitation focus groups with adult participants over the age of 65, along with surveys, interviews with program administrators, and participant observation. Photo elicitation inserts photographs in an interview with the purpose of generating a response (Harper, 2002). Typically, participants take pictures responding to a set of prompts posed by the evaluator. This type of focus group can be a powerful combination to promote self-reflexivity due to photography's power to elicit recall of memories not always accessible through words (Noland, 2006), and a focus group's power to foster the contrast of ideas among participants (Goss & Leinbach, 1996).

The developmental theory used to guide the evaluation was Erik Erikson's psychosocial model of the life cycle, which describes developmental tasks of adulthood (Identity, Intimacy, Generativity, Guardianship, and Integrity), each with "the individual's increasing capacity to relate to an ever-expanding life space of people and institutions" (Vaillant & Milofsky, 1980, p. 1349). Generativity (teaching the next generation) and Guardianship (being a historian for the larger culture) are the two tasks where participants were located.

I conducted three focus groups (~90 minutes), two of them with the same three participants and one with five participants. The participants in the first two focus groups took their own pictures in our first meeting and selected which ones they wanted to talk about in the second focus group. The participants in the third focus group selected their photographs from a set of evaluator-generated images.

The use of printed photographs in focus groups was culturally responsive in two main ways:

- Photo elicitation provided the scaffolding for participants to be self-reflexive about their psychosocial development. Participants situated themselves as Generative teachers who were drawn to teaching the next generation (Erikson, 1967) and passed down the knowledge they acquired through the program for the benefit of the next generation. They also situated themselves as Guardians drawn to preserve their family's history (Vaillant & Milofsky, 1980) through images of the different generations.

- Photo elicitation responded to the cultural meanings of photographs for senior adults, who consider printed photographs as a formal affair to mark special occasions and as keepsakes that are used as a ritual of family unity (Sarvas & Frohlich, 2011; Van House, 2011).

Lessons Learned

The implementation of photo elicitation varied from the first set of focus groups to the second due to logistical considerations, which provided the opportunity to reflect and compare. During data collection, I learned that a third of the 31 program participants suffered cognitive decline. The implications were that a third of participants might need a legal proxy's signed consent to participate in the evaluation, which meant that I might have to destroy their data if I couldn't secure it. After inquiring, the center's leadership assured me that none of the HAP participants had a legal proxy, so the existing informed consent was sufficient. However, my continued interaction with participants indicated that their cognitive function may have been more impaired than the absence of legal proxies might signal. This made me question their actual capacity to provide informed consent to participate in evaluation activities, including photo-elicitation. Thus, using pictures from the participants with cognitive decline raised a dilemma where legality and ethics were not aligned. I decided that I would not use pictures in the evaluation report to avoid direct identification. I also blurred any recognizable faces in pictures that I used in presentations and publications to further protect participants, independently of cognitive decline status. Therefore, evaluators may want to consider the following when working with senior adults:

- Before starting data collection, it would be prudent to check with partners about the cognitive status of potential participants to ensure the implementation of proper consent procedures.

- It may be necessary to take additional measures to protect participants, as the advancement of cognitive decline creates grey areas for participants' ability to provide continued consent.

The original plan was to exclusively use participant-generated photographs. Knowing in advance that participants had physical impairments and cognitive decline, I had planned to accompany them in their picture-taking immediately after the first focus group. However, the focus group ran over time, leaving little time to take pictures before the next activity started. Additionally, participants had difficulties with electronic devices. During the preceding focus group, we had done a picture sort activity with evaluator-generated pictures. Seeing the limitations in time and device manipulation, participants decided to choose images from the picture sort activity to answers my prompts, which meant that the subsequent focus group included both participant- and evaluator-generated pictures. I was first concerned that evaluator-generated photographs would not have the same elicitation power. However, this was not the case, and participants used them to share deeply significant stories. For example, one of the participants used a picture from the picture sort that I took of the group while volunteering at the local food bank to talk about her desire to give back to the community because of all the support that she had received through the years. If we had only used participant-generated pictures, the food bank picture would have been absent and she may have never talked about her urge to give back. Knowing that the second group would include participants with cognitive decline, I decided to exclusively use evaluator-generated photographs. Though I had originally planned to exclusively use participant-generated photographs to center the evaluation around participants' experiences, using evaluator-generated pictures broadened the spectrum of photographs that they could use to talk about their experiences without de-centering their experiences. This experience showed that technology, time, and who generates the pictures are important considerations:

- If evaluators can afford it, it is preferable to use technology that participants are familiar with to prevent technical difficulties that may be accentuated by physical and cognitive impairments.

- Evaluators need to provide sufficient time for participants to take photographs so that they are not limited in terms of time and space.

- Evaluators should also consider the potential impairments of participants and how they may influence their picture-taking and the possibility of using pictures generated by different stakeholders.

Traditionally, photographs had "an emotional and sensory impact beyond that of their content" (Van House, 2011, p. 126) that manifested in their use for archival, display, and story-telling purposes. Participants adhered to this understanding of photographs and preferred having printed copies. Participants' enjoyment of the prints often turned to personally significant moments. In one of these moments, participants were looking in the pictures for one of the members of the center who I was not familiar with. When I inquired, participants told me that she had passed away a few weeks earlier, so they were trying to find pictures of her as keepsakes. Having printed photographs allowed them to reconnect with the people portrayed through embedded memories, emotions, and stories. When evaluators use photoelicitation in their work, they may want to consider the following as they may influence how images are interpreted:

- what the context of generation and use of photographs was

- the significance of the relationship of participants with photography

Discussion Questions

1. What are other potential ethical implications of using photo-elicitation focus groups with senior citizens?

2. When would it be more appropriate to use evaluator- versus participant-generated photographs with adults over 65?

3. What are other elements of photo-elicitation focus groups that could make them culturally responsive to older adults?

References

Adler, G., & Rottunda, S. (2006). Older adults' perspectives on driving cessation. *Journal of Aging Studies, 20*(3), 227–235.

Barrett, J., & Kirk, S. (2000). Running focus groups with elderly and disabled elderly participants. *Applied Ergonomics, 6,* 621.

Basch, C. E. (1987). Focus group interview: An underutilized research technique for improving theory and practice in health education. *Health Education Quarterly, 14*(4), 411–448.

Bloor, M., Frankland, J., Thomas, M., & Robson, K. (2001). *Focus groups in social research.* Thousand Oaks, CA: Sage.

Bokhorst-Heng, W., & Keating Marshall, K. (2019) Informing research (practices) through pedagogical theory: Focus groups with adolescents. *International Journal of Research & Method in Education, 42*(2), 148–162.

Boyce, A. & Chouinard, J. (2017). Moving beyond the buzzword: A framework for teaching culturally responsive approaches to evaluation. *Canadian Journal of Program Evaluation, 32*(2). 266–279.

Brondani, M. A., MacEntee, M. I., Bryant, S. R., & O Neill, B. (2008). Using written vignettes in focus groups among older adults to discuss oral health as a sensitive topic. *Qualitative Health Research, 8,* 1145.

Charlesworth, L. W., & Rodwell, M. K. (1997). Focus groups with children: A resource for sexual abuse prevention program evaluation. *Child Abuse & Neglect, 21*(12), 1205–1216.

Chouinard, J. A. (2014). Understanding relationships in culturally complex evaluation contexts. *Evaluation, 20*(3), 332–347.

Cohen, H. L., Sandel, M. H., Thomas, C. L., & Barton, T. R. (2004). Using focus groups as an educational methodology: Deconstructing stereotypes and social work practice misconceptions concerning aging and older adults. *Educational Gerontology, 30*(4), 329–346.

Cram, F., & Mertens, D. M. (2016). Negotiating solidarity between Indigenous and transformative paradigms in evaluation. *Evaluation Matters—He Take Tō Te Aromatawai, 2,* 161–189.

Danby, S., & Farrell, A. (2004). Accounting for young children's competence in educational research: New perspectives on research ethics. *The Australian Educational Researcher, 31*(3), 35–49.

Darbyshire, P., MacDougall, C., & Schiller, W. (2005). Multiple methods in qualitative research with children: More insight or just more? *Qualitative Research, 5*(4), 417–436.

Davis, A., & Jones, L. (1996). Environmental constraints on health: Listening to children's views. *Health Education Journal, 55,* 363–374.

Delavan, M., Valdez, V., & Freire, J. (2017). Language as whose resource?: When global economics usurp the local equity potentials of dual language education. *International Multilingual Research Journal, 11*(2), 86–100.

Foucault, M. (1982). The subject and power. *Critical Inquiry, 8*(4). 777–795.

Gibson, F. (2007). Conducting focus groups with children and young people: Strategies for success. *Journal of Research in Nursing, 12,* 473–483.

Gonzales, R.G., Suarez-Orozco, C. & Dedios-Sanguineti, M.C. (2013). No place to belong: Contextualizing concepts of mental health among undocumented immigrant youth in the United States. *American Behavior Scientist, 57*(8), 1174–1199.

Greenbaum, T. L. (1990). Focus group support predicted for the '90s. *Marketing News, 24*(1), 21–22.

Greene, J., DeStefano, L., Burgon, H., & Hall, J. N. (2006). An educative, values-engaged approach to evaluating STEM educational programs. In D. Huffman & F. Lawrenz (Eds), *Critical issues in STEM evaluation, New Directions for Evaluation, 109,* (pp. 53–71). San Francisco, CA: Jossey-Bass.

Greene, S., & Hogan, D. (2005). *Researching children's experience: Approaches and methods.* Thousand Oaks, CA: Sage.

Goss, J. D., & Leinbach, T. R. (1996). Focus groups as alternative research practice: Experience with transmigrants in Indonesia. *Area,* 115–123.

Halpin, S. N. (2018). Declining with purpose: Resilience despite cognitive decline. *Life Span Disability, 21*(1), 89–108.

Halpin, S. N., Dillard, R. L., Idler, E., Clevenger, C., Rothschild, E., Blanton, S., & Flacker, J. M. (2017). The benefits of being a senior mentor: Cultivating resilience through the mentorship of health professions students. *Gerontology & Geriatrics Education, 38*(3), 283–294.

Harper, D. (2002). Talking about pictures: A case for photo elicitation. *Visual Studies, 17*(1), 13–26.

Hawthorne, G., Davidson, N., Quinn, K., McCrate, F., Winkler, I., Lucas, R., Molzahn, A. (2006). Issues in conducting cross-cultural research: Implementation of an agreed international protocol designed by the WHOQOL group for the conduct of focus groups eliciting the quality of life of older adults. *Quality of Life Research, 15*(7), 1257.

Hood, S., Hopson, R., & Kirkhart, K. E. (2015). Culturally responsive evaluation. In K. E. Newcomer, H.P. Hatry & J. S Wholey (Eds.), *Handbook of practical program evaluation* (4th ed.) (pp. 281–317). Hoboken, N J: John Wiley & Sons.

Hoppe, M. J., Wells, E. A., Morrison, D.M., Gillmore, M.R., & Wilsdon, A.W. (1995). Using focus groups to discuss sensitive topics with children. *Evaluation Review, 19*(1), 102.

Horner, S. D. (2000). Using focus group methods with middle school children. *Research in Nursing & Health, 23*(6), 510–517.

Jaffe-Walter, R., & Lee, S. (2018). Engaging the transnational lives of immigrant youth in public schooling: Toward a culturally sustaining pedagogy for newcomer immigrant youth. *American Journal of Education, 124*(3), 257–257.

Kirkhart, K. E. (1995). Seeking multicultural validity: A postcard from the road. *Evaluation Practice, 16*, 1–12.

Krause, N., Chatters, L. M., Meltzer, T., & Morgan. D. L. (2000). Negative interaction in the church: Insights from focus groups with older adults. *Review of Religious Research, 41*(4), 510.

Levine, I. S., & Zimmerman, J. D. (1996). Using qualitative data to inform public policy: Evaluating 'Choose to De-Fuse'. *American Journal of Orthopsychiatry, 66*(3), 363.

Malsbary, C. (2014). "It's not just learning English, it's learning other cultures": Belonging, power, and possibility in an immigrant contact zone. *International Journal of Qualitative Studies in Education, 27*(10), 1312–1336.

Mauthner, M. (1997). Methodological aspects of collecting data from children: Lessons from three research projects. *Children & Society, 11*(1), 16–28.

Melenhorst, A.S., Rogers, W. A., & Bouwhuis, D. G. (2006). Older adults' motivated choice for technological innovation: Evidence for benefit-driven selectivity. *Psychology and Aging, 1*, 190.

Mertens, D. M. (2014). *Research and evaluation in education and psychology: Integrating diversity with quantitative, qualitative, and mixed methods.* Thousand Oaks, CA: Sage.

Mishna, F., Saini, M., & Solomon, S. (2009). Ongoing and online: Children and youths' perceptions of cyber bullying. *Children and Youth Services Review, 31*(12), 1222–1228.

Mitzner, T. L., Boron, J. B., Fausset, C. B., Adams, A. E., Charness, N., Czaja, S. J., & Sharit, J. (2010). Older adults talk technology: Technology usage and attitudes. *Computers in Human Behavior, 26*, 1710–1721.

Morgan, D. (2019). *Basic and advanced focus groups.* Thousand Oaks, CA: Sage.

Morgan, M., Gibbs, S., Maxwell, K., & Britten, N. (2002). Hearing children's voices: Methodological issues in conducting focus groups with children aged 7-11 years. *Qualitative Research, 2*(1), 5–20.

Morrison, D., Lichtenwald, K., & Tang, R. (2019). Extending the online focus group method using web-based conferencing to explore older adults online learning. *International Journal of Research & Method in Education, 1*–15.

Noland, C. M. (2006). Auto-photography as research practice: Identify and self-esteem research. *Journal of Research Practice, 2*(1),

Northridge, M., Shedlin, M., Schrimshaw, E., Estrada, I., Da La Cruz, L., Peralta, R., Bridsall, S., Metcaff, S., Chakraborty, B., & Kunzel, C. (2017). Recruitment of racial/ethnic minority older adults through community sites for focus group discussions. *BMC Public Health, 17*(1).

Oakley, A. (1994). Women and children first and last: Parallels and differences between children and women's studies. In B. Mayal (Ed.), *Children's childhoods observed and experienced* (pp. 13–32). Thousand Oaks, CA: Sage.

Orellana, M. (2009). *Translating childhoods: Immigrant youth, language, and culture.* New Brunswick, NJ: Rutgers University Press.

Quine, S., & Cameron, I. (1995). The use of focus groups with the disabled elderly. *Qualitative Health Research, 4,* 454.

Reyes, C. (2019). An English learner as a cultural broker for youth interviews. *Qualitative Report, 24*(3), 532.

Rodriguez, S. (2019). "We're building the community; It's a hub for democracy": Lessons learned from a library-based program for newcomer immigrant and refugee youth. *Children and Youth Services Review, 102,* 135–144.

Rodriguez, S., Naficy, H., & Russo, M. (2020). "It's a hub for democracy": How a library-based program increases belonging for newcomer immigrant and refugee youth. In Ana Ndumu (Ed), *Borders & belonging: Critical examinations of LIS approaches toward immigrants.* Sacramento, CA: Litwin Books/ Library Juice Press.

Reichstadt, J., Depp, C. A., Palinkas, L. A., Folsom D. P., & Jeste, D. V. (2007). Building blocks of successful aging: A focus group study of older adults' perceived contributors to successful aging. *American Journal of Geriatric Psychiatry, 15*(3), 194–201.

Sarvas, R., & Frohlich, D. M. (2011). *From snapshots to social media. The changing picture of domestic photography.* London: Springer.

Sugarman, J., McCrory, D. C., and Hubal, R. C. (1998). Getting meaningful informed consent from older adults: A structured literature review of empirical research. *Journal of the American Geriatrics Society, 46*(4), 517–524.

Vaillant, G. E., & Milofsky, E. (1980). Natural history of male psychological health: IX. Empirical evidence for Erikson's model of the life cycle. *The American Journal of Psychiatry, 137*(11), 1348–1359.

Van House, N. A. (2011). Personal photography, digital technologies and the uses of the visual. *Visual Studies, 26*(2), 125–134.

CHAPTER SIX

Indigenous- and Feminist-Oriented Focus Groups

In This Chapter

- Indigenous-Oriented Focus Groups

  - Ethical Considerations

  - A Case Example: Fa'afaletui: A Mat Woven Through Many Houses

  - Summary

- Feminist-Oriented Focus Groups

  - Ethical Considerations

  - A Case Example: Feminist-Intersectional Focus Groups

  - Summary

IN THIS CHAPTER, I discuss culturally responsive focus groups from In-digenous- and feminist-oriented perspectives. While theoretically distinct, both orientations critique traditional Western methodologies (Prasad, 2018) and seek to dismantle current sociocultural hierarchies, bringing "knowledge of and from the margins to the centre" (Parashar, 2016, p. 371). While it is beyond the scope of this book to provide a comprehensive review of Indigenous or feminist perspectives or focus group strategies for each type of Indigenous or feminist group, this chapter does afford insights into some approaches taken to develop and implement focus groups in ways that aim to honor the ambitions of both orientations. To further demonstrate how culturally responsive inquirers can take Indigenous and feminist orientations into account, two case examples are offered. The first illustrates a non-Western focus group method, *fa'afaletui*. The second case example illustrates a feminist-oriented focus group drawing on Crenshaw's (1989) concept of intersectionality.

Indigenous-Oriented Focus Groups

There was, and remains, serious concern about the legacy of colonialism. As discussed in Chapter 1, researchers from the West who traveled to colonized countries studied cultures of different communities, often objectifying and positioning the ethnic or cultural *Other* as comparatively deficient. As a result, the research methods used became linked to the colonial agenda (Denzin, Lincoln, & Smith, 2008). It is against this legacy of colonialism that Indigenous-oriented research has emerged, and continues to emerge (Kovach, 2018). Indigenous-oriented research is an overarching term including various Indigenous methodological orientations that attempt to dismantle the colonial agenda (Kovach, 2018). However, it should be noted that the term Indigenous is not without controversy, as there is no single Indigenous group and some groups prefer the use of other terms (i.e., Aboriginal, First Nation) (Peters & Mika, 2017). That said, Indigenous peoples have been described as

> inheritors and practitioners of unique cultures and ways of relating to people and the environment. They have retained social, cultural, economic and political characteristics that are distinct from those of the dominant societies in which they live. Despite their cultural difference, Indigenous peoples from around the world share common problems related to the protection of their rights as distinct peoples. (United Nations, 2019)

Recognizing the unique cultures of various groups, Indigenous-oriented research strives to center and honor these groups' distinct knowledges, practices, traditions, and worldviews (Denzin, Lincoln, & Smith, 2008; Kovach, 2018). Indigenous-oriented research also attempts to counter narratives of Indigenous deficiency by conducting research in collaboration with Indigenous communities, engaging issues and topics of benefit to them (Denzin, Lincoln, & Smith, 2008; Kovach, 2018). This means that careful consideration must be given to *whether* and *how* Western methods such as focus groups should be implemented in Indigenous contexts. For instance, South African scholars Khupe and Keane (2017) assert that traditional focus groups were appropriate for their participatory science education research projects conducted in rural South African communities as the focus group structure follows the format of Traditional Council meetings. However, that is a unique context; focus groups may be inappropriate in other Indigenous settings. Checking the suitability of focus groups for a particular Indigenous context is especially important to ensure that its utilization will contribute "to the decolonization, equity, and social justice for Indigenous peoples" (Cram, 2018, p. 131). *Indigenous-oriented focus groups*, then, as I am defining them, include traditional focus groups that are informed by, or aligned with, Indigenous ways of knowing—as in the Khupe and Keane (2017) example above—and non-Western methods developed by particular Indigenous groups (Kovach, 2018).

Indigenous Ways of Knowing. Conducting Indigenous-oriented focus groups requires an understanding of Indigenous ways of knowing, which include beliefs or assumptions about the nature of knowledge and how one comes to understand the world (Denzin, Lincoln, & Smith 2008; Kovach, 2018; Smith, 2000). Table 6.1 *Tenets of Indigenous Knowledge*, outlines the tenets of Indigenous knowledge and a brief description of each as articulated by Kovach (2018, p. 218).

"Indigenous ways of knowing" also includes the sociopolitical history and current context of an Indigenous community. Reservations, provinces, urban areas, rural villages, and international settings are just some examples of Indigenous contexts. Each context has distinctive historical, spiritual, social, political, legal and governance characteristics. For example, according to the National Congress of American Indians (2019), "there are 573 federally recognized Indian Nations (variously called tribes, nations, bands, pueblos, communities and native villages) in the United States," reflecting a wide range of linguistic and ethnic diversity. Each Nation is sovereign with

Table 6.1: *Tenets of Indigenous Knowledge*

Tenet of Indigenous Knowledge	Description
Knowledge is holistic and implies empirical, experiential, sensory, and metaphysical possibilities	Recognizes there is no separation between humans and the universe
Knowledge arises from interconnectivity and interdependency	Reflects the belief that knowledge stems from being in relation with others and is associated with values of reciprocity and responsibility
Knowledge is animate and fluid	Treats knowledge as dynamic, shifting as understandings of the world change
Knowledge arises from a multiplicity of sources, including nonhuman sources	Acknowledges how spiritual energy connects life forms and contributes to understanding the world

the power to determine its own governance structures (National Congress of American Indians, 2019). Whereas having a general understanding of Indigenous ways of knowing, and context, is important, conducting Indigenous-oriented focus groups also necessitates comprehending the particular Indigenous principles associated with an Indigenous community.

Indigenous Principles. Indigenous communities have distinct cultures, including their own practices and values. These practices and values or *Indigenous principles* are context-specific and reflect the life experiences of an Indigenous group (Kovach, 2018). When conducting focus groups with Māori in Aotearoa (New Zealand), for example, Smith (1999) suggests that researchers follow a *kaupapa* Māori approach:

1. *Aroha kit te tangata* (respect for people)

2. *Kanohi kitea* ("the seen face," that is, present yourself to people face-to-face)

3. *Titiro, whakarongo…korero* (look, listen…speak)

4. *Manaaki kit e tangata* (share and host people, be generous)

5. *Kia tupato* (be cautious)

6. *Kaua e takahia te mana o te tangata* (do not trample over the *mana* of people)

7. *Kaua e mahaki* (don't flaunt your knowledge) (p. 120)

While principles do not capture *all* the values and practices of an Indigenous culture, they do provide basic guidelines for how to govern relationships with people in that context (Smith, 1999). Using Indigenous principles to guide focus group development and implementation helps to ensure the focus groups are culturally congruent with the distinct Indigenous community you seek to work with.

Forms of Indigenous-oriented Focus Groups. As mentioned earlier, I define Indigenous-oriented focus groups as including two forms (1) traditional focus groups that are informed by or aligned with Indigenous knowledge systems, and (2) non-Western focus group methods. Fa'afaletui is an example of a non-Western approach to focus groups. Specifically, it is a Samoan-derived method for collecting and validating knowledge (Tamasese, Peteru, Waldegrave, & Bush, 2004). It was initially used to gather Samoan perspectives on mental health services and is now used with Pan-Pacific persons (Tamasese et al., 2004). To implement fa'afaletui one must be aware of the principles central to Samoan culture. One such principle is the belief of self as a relational being, which implies a person is not separate from others in the community and suggests relationships are sacred and guided by cultural codes of conduct. These codes of conduct define how certain groups (i.e., Elders, siblings) should relate to each other; thereby protecting the well-being of the overall community (Tamasese et al., 2004). The case example in Box 6.1 *Fa'afaletui: A Mat Woven Through Many Houses* presented later in the chapter, illustrates the implementation of Samoan principles central to fa'afaletui.

Cross-cultural Misunderstandings. Cross-cultural focus groups increase the chances of misunderstandings during the session as well as subsequent misinterpretations of focus group data. Therefore, offering opportunities for stakeholders to check cultural interpretations becomes even more important (Dawson et al., 2014; Waapalaneexkweew [Bowman, N., Mohican/Lunaape] & Dodge-Francis, C., 2018). To check for understanding, a synthesis and validation of ideas and concepts are recommended (Halcomb et al. (2007). To permit synthesis and validation of Indigenous perceptions during the focus group, researchers often summarize key points throughout the focus group and/or at the end, asking participants to confirm the accuracy of the points made (DiGiacomo et al., 2013). Researchers have also shared written preliminary reports, including summary "highlights" with focus group participants to check the accuracy of interpretations based on the focus group data (Romm, 2018). To further validate participants' ideas and stories, researchers have followed up with participants for clarification and feedback, leading to a more in-depth understanding of participants' perceptions and issues (Romm, 2018).

Empowerment. While having Indigenous focus group participants check preliminary findings is certainly helpful, incorporating opportunities for Indigenous communities to work collaboratively during the entire research is critically imperative and potentially empowering. For example, in a study investigating natural resources in Miskito and Mayangna communities in Nicaragua, community members were given opportunities to be treated as experts in their community, make decisions about data collection, and judge the accuracy and completeness of the data (Danielson et al., 2014). Ultimately, having control over the focus group data collection and its subsequent use is vital to a community's sense of empowerment (Halcomb et al., 2007; Danielson et al., 2014).

Focus Group Environment. Attempts to ensure the focus group takes place in a non-threatening environment are especially important when conducting focus groups with Indigenous communities (Martin, 2008). One option for a comfortable setting is to conduct the focus group where participants are accustomed to meeting (Halcomb et al., 2007, p. 1004). For instance, in a study investigating the perspectives of caregivers and health providers on Aboriginal childhood disability services, the researchers secured a familiar community facility to conduct their focus group sessions (DiGiacomo et al., 2013). In addition, the environment of the focus group includes seating arrangements. Whereas the circular Western-style arrangement of traditional focus groups may work for some non-Western participants, other cultural groups may feel less comfortable with this arrangement (Halcomb et al., 2007). For example,

> Asian style focus group customarily provide desks or tables for participants because a barrier placed in front of a person is a welcome physical defense. Without this physical barrier, many participants would feel uncomfortable which might, therefore, hinder openness rather than enhance it. (p. 1004)

Focus Group Workshops, Training, and Team Meetings. Many Indigenous communities have been disempowered in their relationships with Western researchers and evaluators. One strategy used to strengthen relationships with Indigenous communities is to hold focus group training workshops (Pere & Barnes, 2009; Romm, 2018; Waapalaneexkweew [Bowman] & Dodge-Francis, 2018). Romm (2018) describes the focus group training sessions provided for 46 university researchers to study an educational invention in South Africa. She explains that these focus group training workshops were advantageous for planning how to collaborate with participants, and encouraged them to share potential solutions to issues identified. Another example comes from Waapalaneexkweew (Bowman) and Dodge-Francis' (2018) evaluation that describes the training provided to a 26-member evaluation team responsible for assessing the ability of Tribal governments and Indigenous communities in the United States to direct their nutrition programs. For this training,

> pre-reading materials were given to the training participants a week in advance and a full-day online and interactive webinar training was provided to cover CBPR [community-based participatory research], TDPR [Tribally Driven Participatory Research], Tribal governance and sovereignty, an overview of the historical and cultural aspects of Indigenous populations, governance and operational differences of Tribes an Tribal nonprofits, and human, cultural, and intellectual property protections via Tribal IRBs. (p. 24)

Although the training activities described by Waapalaneexkweew (Bowman) and Dodge-Francis (2018) were intended for a culturally responsive Indigenous evaluation that did not include focus groups, the specific strategies mentioned are helpful to consider how training sessions can be used to inform team members about the different aspects of the Indigenous contexts they will engage. Also, both Romm (2018) and Waapalaneexkweew (Bowman) and Dodge-Francis (2018) mention how additional team member meetings were held throughout their investigations to further support respectful relationships with Indigenous stakeholders and address questions that arose.

Focus Group Composition. When determining the composition of focus groups, it is important to be aware of any cultural principles or codes of conduct related to gender, status, age and so on that dictate how different groups of people within the Indigenous community are to be in relation with each other (Halcomb et al., 2007). Such cultural principles inform how you will need to divide or segment groups (Morgan, 2019). For example, segmentation was used to study an educational intervention in Africa including diverse participants who ranged in age and status (Romm, 2018). Focus group participants in this study were separated into four categories: (1) school governing bodies (SGBs) and parents/guardians who were not members of SGBs; (2) school management teams; (3) teachers; and (4) learners (Grades 3 and 6) (Romm, 2018). Segmenting by categories in this context promoted the comfort of participants, particularly for those having the least power. For instance, not being in the presence of teachers enabled students in grades 3 and 6 to more fully and freely express themselves (Romm, 2018).

Focus Group Participation. Indigenous ways of knowing values being in relation with others. Seeking ways to enhance Indigenous participants' involvement in focus groups honors this perspective. To encourage participation, some practical advice is offered. First, consult with Indigenous leaders in the community to understand holidays, rituals, ceremonies or certain days of the week that may create barriers to participation when scheduling focus groups (Colucci, 2008, p. 239). Second, involve participants in the development of focus group questions (Colucci, 2008, p. 241). This will help to ensure that the topics and issues discussed are relevant and of interest to Indigenous participants. Third, understand the type of focus group style the Indigenous community would like to use (Colucci, 2008). Whereas the narrative and collective style of focus groups is congruent with the storytelling styles of many Indigenous communities (Gorman & Toombs, 2009), approaches to engaging Indigenous participants in discussion differ greatly, ranging from formal to informal styles (Halcomb et al., 2007). For example, *yarning* has been described as a more culturally suitable focus group style to privilege Aboriginal knowledge (Dawson et al., 2014). Also, encouraging participation may include having additional time for the focus group discussion to allow for prayers or other cultural practices (Halcomb et al., 2007, p. 1007).

Moderating Focus Groups. Implementing focus groups in a different cultural context may require using the Indigenous language of the participants. If the moderator is unable to speak the mother tongue of focus group participants, then an interpreter will be needed. In practice, this could mean that Indigenous and non-Indigenous researchers/moderators work through simultaneous translation during a focus group session (DiGiacomo et al., 2013). Romm (2018), an English speaker, describes how the focus group sessions in her project were conducted by both "Zulu and English-speaking facilitators, with Zulu speaking ones translating into English from time to time" (p. 976). The English translations of participants' responses during the focus group allowed Romm (2018) to probe or ask follow up questions. If the moderator is unable to speak the language of the Indigenous group, another option is to have an interpreter carry out the entire focus group. Also, having a note taker present to take notes throughout the focus group meeting (Colucci, 2008; DiGiacomo et al., 2013) is helpful for capturing participants' verbal and nonverbal responses, leading to additional Indigenous insights. Yet, it should be mentioned that taking notes or recording during the focus group can be deemed culturally insensitive in some non-Western contexts (See case example in Box 6.1 *Fa'afaletui: A Mat Woven Through Many Houses* for example.)

Recruitment and Incentives. Many researchers use snowball sampling to recruit Indigenous participants as they are more likely to participate based on the recommendation of a person in their community (Colucci, 2008). Other recruitment methods include flyers, and sending announcements to relevant organizations. For instance, DiGiacomo, Delaney, Abbott, Davidson, Delany and Vincent (2013) report that to understand health care services of Aboriginal children with a disability, flyers were posted in an Aboriginal Community Controlled Health Service (ACCHS) and emails were sent to "relevant professional groups and disability networks within three proximal health district areas, or given directly to community members by Aboriginal Health Workers (AHWs) or ACCHS staff" (p. 3). In terms of incentive, providing food or some sort of refreshment is recommended (Colucci, 2008) when conducting focus groups with *some* Indigenous groups. However, researchers will need to carefully consider at what point (before, during or after the focus group) to provide food, if at all (Colucci, 2008).

Ethical Considerations

Historical discrimination and marginalization have contributed to fear and mistrust of research and evaluation among many Indigenous communities. Therefore, to conduct focus groups in an ethically responsible manner, it is necessary to understand an Indigenous group's particular history. Here, having Indigenous stakeholders assist when developing and implementing focus groups becomes extremely important to ensure culturally safe practices (Dawson et al., 2014). Related to this point, understanding guidelines for how the focus group data should be handled and protected is also imperative for ethical practice. Some countries such as Brazil, Peru, Panama, and the Philippines, for example, have

> laws which regulate access to genetic resources and empower indigenous peoples to implement their own customary law obligations, and confer upon traditional owners the right to prevent others from reproducing and misappropriating traditional indigenous knowledge. (Kariyawasam & Guy, 2007, p. 106)

Summary

The diversity of Indigenous peoples demands attention to their unique cultural, socioeconomic-political contexts. Both kinds of Indigenous-oriented focus groups—traditional focus groups informed by Indigenous principles as well as Indigenous methods (i.e., fa'afaletui)—seek to recognize the distinct orientations of Indigenous groups by advancing Indigenous knowledge and empowerment. The responsive and ethical implementation of Indigenous-oriented focus groups rests on engaging the historical and contemporary context of Indigenous peoples, collaborating with Indigenous communities, and countering deficit-based Indigenous discourses (Ossai, 2010; Owusu-Ansah & Miji, 2013; Waapalaneexkweew [Bowman] & Dodge-Francis, 2018; Cram, 2018).

The case example in Box 6.1: *Fa'afaletui: A Mat Woven Through Many Houses* takes a close look at a culturally responsive project that incorporated fa'afaletui, a non-Western approach to focus groups (Tamasese, Peteru, Waldegrave, & Bush, 2004). Of notable interest are how the principles of the Samoan culture were upheld in Fa'afaletui as well as the inherent complexities of working across different cultures (Samoan, Māori, Pakeha, United States) and disciplines (mental health, public health, community development, social policy development) in an international context.

Box 6.1 *Fa'afaletui: A Mat Woven Through Many Houses*

Fa'afaletui: A Mat Woven Through Many Houses
By Lorien S. Jordan, PhD, LMFT

In New Zealand, *Pasifikas* are people who are either Pacific Island-born or New Zealand-born who identify with a Pacific heritage (Mila-Schaaf & Hudson, 2009). While Pasifikas represent a wide range of cultures, many share similar views of collective belonging and connected wellbeing. This sense of belonging was the focus of one aspect of an international investigation of marginalization and health outcomes in Indigenous communities.

The project took place in New Zealand, a settler-colonial country, that seeks amelioration of the effects of colonization on Māori (Indigenous peoples of New Zealand) and areas throughout the Pacific Ocean (e.g., Samoa, Tokelau). Culture in New Zealand largely reflects a melding of the dominant population of Pakeha (New Zealanders of European descent) and Māori. However, given that many of the Pacific Islands were colonized by, are accessible to and, in some ways, dependent on New Zealand there is a sizeable transnational population of Pasifikas. The New Zealand-specific arm of the larger international study comprised two parallel investigations of Māori and Pasifika health. The following case review provides a brief description of the Pan-Pacific design of the New Zealand study. To honor the collective identities of Pasifika peoples, we engaged in *fa'afaletui*, a non-Western approach to focus groups developed by, and for, Pasifikas in New Zealand (Tamasese, Peteru, & Waldegrave, 1999).

The theoretical orientation of fa'afaletui is inherently Indigenous and was devised by Samoans, for research with Samoan and other Pasifika peoples. Decolonizing theory also informed the development of this project, as in New Zealand colonialism is an ongoing reality and decolonizing remains an unfinished business (Smith, 2012). Decolonialism deconstructs how the legacies of Imperialism have unequally divided human social, cultural, political, spiritual, and economic capital (Smith, 2012). The central goal of decolonizing Pasifika research is to decenter Western knowledge systems, through privileging Pan-Pacific ontologies and cosmologies.

Fa'afaletui is a culturally derived Indigenous qualitative methodology method, reflective of values and structures within Samoan communities (Tamasese, Peteru, & Waldegrave, 1999). It attends to a Samoan view of the self, which constituted in the *va*, which is a relational space wherein one's identity has meaning only in relationship. Focus groups are the primary data collection method in fa'afaletui, to create the space of va with participants. Fa'afaletui also acknowledges the significance of Pasifika oral traditions. Focus groups can facilitate the multidirectional gifting of knowledge between cultures and identities facilitated. This is the process of *tui*: weaving together findings, as one would a straw mat. Weaving is a metaphor of respect for the uniqueness of each perspective while drawing consensus between and within groups.

The fa'afaletui occurred within a local community development and family therapy agency. Reflecting the interconnected nature of Pasifika wellbeing, the project was carried out by researchers in multiple disciplines including mental health, public health, community development, and social policy development. The researchers also represented different cultures, including Samoan, Māori, Pakeha, and that of the author, who is from the United States.

A total of 28 members from Samoan, Tokelauan, Tongan, and Cook Island communities participated. Male ($n = 13$) and female ($n = 15$) participants from a range of ages contributed to the fa'afaletui; the youngest member was 16 and the eldest 71. Within these groups, members were both island-born and New Zealand-born.

Fa'afaletui for this project were organized in three waves, organizing participants according to cultural identity and protocols so that each group represented a *fale* (house). We began with four cultural identity fale, comprised of Samoan (n = 10), Tokelauan (n = 6), Tongan (n = 8), and Cook Island (n = 4) community members, to discuss the differences and similarities between Pasifika cultures. Following the first round of focus groups, the different cultural members were brought together and organized into fale of Elder women (n= 8), Elder men (n = 7), young adult women (n = 7), and young adult men (n = 6). Genders were separated according to cultural protocols, ensuring that topics considered *tapu* (forbidden or sacred) for discussion across genders, were discussed freely. Age was another distinction, as *matua* (eldership) status is a position of standing that carries significant roles and responsibilities for the continuation of culture. In the last wave, representatives from each fale came together to weave the findings from previous groups.

In each fale, questions asked followed a semi-structured interview guide. Respecting cultural protocols such as not rushing participants, and providing hospitality, were vital to the success of the project. Each meeting lasted from two to three hours, which included prayers, sharing a meal, and time for friendly conversation. The focus groups took place in English, yet many times participants used terms and common vernacular of their languages. The focus groups were not recorded, and instead, extensive notes were taken.

Data analysis followed the approach designed by the originators of fa'afaletui. Following a systematic coding process, the analysis highlighted significant clusters and themes within each fale, then in comparison across fale. Many of the Pasifika languages tend towards metaphor, so to aid in accurate analyses, interpretations were member checked. Throughout the analysis, the fale were brought back together to draw consensus from the interpretations. As findings were agreed to, representatives from each fale contributed to the last round of member checking. Beyond extensive member checking, to ensure credibility, focus groups were facilitated by a cultural representative of each *fale* and accompanied by researchers. Results from the fa'afaletui led to the development of culturally appropriate interview guides, surveys, recruitment procedures, and incentives to inform the larger project design.

Lessons Learned

It is difficult to pull apart the strengths and limitations of fa'afaletui, as they are tightly woven together, much like the tui (mat) represented by this method. First, researchers must enter with cultural humility, as the strengths of fa'afaletui are in its decentering and challenging of Western-based academics. Durie (2011) suggests Indigenous peoples speak and think centrifugally, in a process where people come to conclusions through outward and circular conversation between peoples. This thinking stands counter to the centripetal (e.g., internalized and individualized) thinking, often prioritized in the West. For Pan-Pacific peoples, centrifugal thought is often accompanied by a non-linear view of time. These two elements can provoke challenges for researchers who privilege a linear speaking style and linear time. Research conducted on tight deadlines, and with limited funding, can promote a data extraction mentality, converse to fa'afaletui. To conduct fa'afaletui, hours are spent in fale, in centrifugal discussions marked by allusive and metaphoric speech. The indirect and oral traditions of Samoan and Pasifika cultures are characterized by subtleties and cultural cues. These methods of speech can be difficult for researchers from the United States who can privilege assertive and direct speech. Admittedly, these are cultural generalizations just as there are Pasifikas who speak directly, think centripetally, and embrace a linear concept of time, there are persons from the United States who think collectively, centrifugally, and embrace a non-linear conception of time. What is important is that when researchers enter fa'afaletui, they are aware of, and honor, possible differences.

To me, a scholar trained in the United States, this methodology appeared simultaneously systematic and messy. Certain changes I would make were based on my desire to control processes, such as recording the fale discussions. However, for all the messiness encountered, I would not change the fa'afaletui. Ultimately, I came to understand that the moments when things felt "messy," were the moments I ran into my culturally-bound biases.

Ethical Considerations

To ethically engage with the Pasifika communities in fa'afaletui, time must be spent within the community. Knowledge is not a commodity but a shared gift. Entering a community to extract information in the furtherance of one's own goal would reproduce colonial processes. Developing a fa'afaletui that benefits both researcher and community is critical, as is developing relationships with matua (elders) who are willing to facilitate as cultural brokers. Without attending to these elements, one risks violating cultural protocols and transgressing into the tapu.

Discussion Question

1. To conduct fa'afaletui, Western-trained academics must relinquish the expert role to center the cultural-protocols of Pasifika methodologists. What are some processes that researchers could use to challenge and maintain awareness of their own biases and assumptions, throughout the research?

Feminist-Oriented Focus Groups

Feminism, although described in many ways, can be characterized as a concern for "women's lives and the role of gender in structuring different aspects in society" (Prasad, 2018, p. 181). The tradition of feminism emerged in response to women being exploited in both public (i.e., workplace) and private (i.e., home life) settings (Prasad, 2018). Although initially a sociopolitical movement, feminism has evolved and is now featured in numerous disciplines such as anthropology, health, and education (Harding, 1991; Prasad, 2018).

Focus groups have been found useful by feminist scholars to explore a wide range of topics such as the fear of crime among Latina women (Madriz, 1998) and the role of gender, race, and class in criminal prosecution of females (Pollack, 2003). The studies conducted by feminist scholars in these different contexts illustrate how focus groups are valuable to counter deficit-oriented models of women (Pollack, 2003) and allow them to engage in a more equal relationship with investigators (Madriz, 1998; Wilkinson, 1999). In these ways, *feminist-oriented focus groups* provide a social context for authentic, contextualized and non-exploitative meaning-making for women (Wilkinson, 1999). Yet, it should be made clear that there is no single feminist orientation. Feminism, like other theories, reflects a family of perspectives and orientations. A discussion later in the chapter highlights this point, bringing attention to one particular feminist orientation: Black feminist thought. However, like other traditions, feminism is not without critique. Among the critiques faced by the feminist tradition is its treatment of women as a monolithic group with the same history of subjugation and exploitation (Prasad, 2018). Put differently, a major issue with feminism, according to some scholars, is its lack of engagement of cultural diversity (i.e., race, class, ethnicity, sexual orientation, religion) among women (Prasad, 2018). In response to such critiques, variants of feminism have emerged. These perspectives (i.e., anarchist feminism, Jewish feminism, ecology-focus feminism) reflect different feminist orientations or theories (Harding, 1991), which may guide the development of focus groups.

Feminist Orientations. As a culturally responsive inquirer, you will need to determine the most appropriate feminist orientation to inform the development of your focus groups. Doing so is especially important from a culturally responsive perspective as feminist-oriented focus groups are not simply focus groups designed to include women. Rather, they center women's voices and seek to empower women, as well as examine and confront systems of oppression and how they relate to social identities (i.e., gender, race, sexuality, and class) (Carbado et al., 2013; Collins, 2000; Pollack, 2003; Wilkinson, 1999). One notable and established feminist orientation is Black feminist thought.

Black Feminist Thought. Black feminist thought is a critical social theory that argues Black women are self-defined and independent people with the capacity to confront oppression and use their knowledge as a source of social justice (Collins, 1990). Generally, Black feminist thought is concerned with the "matrix of domination" or the system of oppression (economic, political and ideological) at the intersections of race, class and gender (Collins, 2000). The importance of understanding these intersections was further advanced by Kimberlé Crenshaw's (1989) introduction of *intersectionality* (Crenshaw, 1989), a conceptual framework which was initially used to investigate how structures of power simultaneously interact with the cultural identities of Black women in the context of the United States (Carbado, Crenshaw, Mays, & Tomlinson, 2013). Although anchored in Black feminism and critical race theory, intersectionality is currently employed with other cultural groups to explore a "range of issues, social identities, power dynamics, legal and political systems, and discursive structures in the United

States and beyond" (Carbado, Crenshaw, Mays, & Tomlinson, 2013, p. 304). For instance, Boogaard and Roggeband (2010) used an intersectional lens to guide their case study, including four focus groups with ethnic majority women, ethnic majority men, ethnic minority women and ethnic minority men to investigate the intersections of gender, ethnic, and organizational identities within the context of the Dutch police force.

Forms of Feminist-oriented Focus Groups. Different feminist orientations have led some researchers to reframe focus groups to fit the culture of the women's group they intend to engage. This reframing has resulted in different forms of feminist-oriented focus groups. One such form is *sista circles*. Sista circles acknowledge the culture of Black women, how they communicate, how they are in relation with each other, and their meaning-making processes (Brown, 2019; Johnson, 2015). Sista circles do not represent an entirely new method as they are anchored in the tradition of how Black women have found community and support among themselves in groups for over 150 years (Neal-Barnett, Stadulis, Murray, Payne, Thomas, & Salley, 2011) in response to being excluded from social settings dominated by White females and Black males (Johnson, 2015). As a qualitative research method, sista circles involve a discussion among Black women to explore and examine their issues and or experiences (Johnson, 2015).

Culturally responsive investigators have used sista circles to gain in-depth knowledge of Black women's experiences and advance the empowerment of Black women (Johnson, 2015). For other investigations that used sista circles methodology see (Neal-Barnett et al., 2011; Collier, 2017; Lacy, 2017). A case example included in Appendix B. *Using Sista Circles to Conduct Research About and With Sista Scholars* demonstrates how sista circles were used to explore the experiences of first-generation Black women in their doctoral programs. The discussion on sista circles is not meant to imply that all focus groups with Black women are, or should be, sista circles. Furthermore, the discussion on sista circles highlights *one* type of feminist-oriented focus group approach. There are other forms of feminist-oriented focus groups. For example, Madriz (1998) conceptualizes her focus groups with Latina women as a form of *collective testimony*. Madriz describes collective testimony as a

> sensitive tool to recover and use the knowledge acquired from
> women's subjective experiences of everyday life. These collective

testimonies provide women with the possibility of breaking the wall
of silence that has suppressed the expression of their ideas and emotions. (p. 116)

Like sista circles, collective testimony provides a way for women to be affirmed and empowered by recognizing how their experiences and problems
are shared by other women with a similar ethnic background.

Focus Group Environment. A non-threatening focus group environment is especially important when conducting focus groups with women
from oppressed groups whose voices are often invalidated in social settings.
To enable a nonthreatening environment, researchers commonly opt for
surroundings that are familiar such as church basements, classrooms, the
home of the focus group moderator and community centers (Lee-Lin, Menon, Nail, & Lutz, 2012; Madriz, 1998). When deciding where the focus
groups will be held, there are a couple of additional points to consider. First,
some women participants will attend focus group sessions with their children. Therefore, the moderator will need to consider accommodations for
childcare. Second, some situations necessitate conducting a focus group in
an environment that is unavoidably threatening as was the case in Pollack's
(2003) study which included focus groups with women in a correctional
facility. Yet, while conducting focus groups in a context that amplifies issues
of power is not ideal, Pollack's (2003) focus group example suggests that
opportunities for cultural responsiveness can still be identified. The following section provides an example of this point.

Focus Group Segmentation. On occasion, segmentation is appropriate
when conducting feminist-oriented focus groups. For example, in Pollack's
(2003) study conducted in a women's correctional facility, 15 life-history interviews and three focus groups were used to investigate the impact of gender, race, and class on women's lawbreaking. One of the three focus groups
conducted in prison consisted of four Black Canadian women. Pollack
(2003) explains that the inclusion of a focus group with only Black women
was important to "increase the likelihood that they would speak more freely
about the impact of race and culture, as they were being interviewed by a
White researcher" (p. 465). Pollack (2003) reports how the Black women
in the focus group did indeed discuss how racism negatively influenced their

access to resources (i.e., childcare, affordable housing) and, as a result, led to their lawbreaking. Pollack's study is instructive because it calls attention to how segmentation was helpful to have Black Canadian women engage in a collective dialogue on sensitive topics (i.e., racism, lawbreaking). Furthermore, her study underscores how researchers from a dominant group can thoughtfully conduct culturally responsive focus groups with participants from non-dominant groups.

Focus Group Participation. As mentioned before, women have different cultures and perspectives. Within these different cultures, women have multiple identities and responsibilities. Depending on the cultural context, these responsibilities can make it difficult for some women to participate in focus group sessions. For example, in her study on the fear of crime among Latina women, Madriz (1998) notes that "given women's role in traditional Latino culture, most of them are exclusively responsible for the care of the children and the house" (p. 120). Because of this, it was difficult for the Latina women, especially those with lower incomes, in Madriz's (1998) study to attend focus group sessions. In response, Madriz (1998) coordinated transportation for participants or reimbursed transportation costs. In addition, Madriz (1998) indicated to potential participants that the focus groups would be conducted in Spanish. This form of linguistic responsiveness was imperative because, as Madriz (1998) points out, it was "only after it was conveyed to them that the conversation was going to be in Spanish did they agree to participate" (p. 123).

Moderating Focus Groups. Moderators of feminist-oriented focus groups are charged with facilitating empathetic and collaborative interactions that enable self-disclosure, the identification of common experiences across participants and the validation of women's stories (Madriz, 1998). To encourage this type of interaction, some researchers identified moderators who have experience conducting focus groups with women as well as familiarity with the specific context (Lee-Lin et al., 2012; Thomas et al., 2014). For instance, Thomas et al., (2014) states focus groups used to examine a health intervention for Black women were led by facilitators with experience running focus groups with women in a health care setting. Other culturally responsive inquirers consider conducting focus groups with a female moderator of the same linguistic background as focus groups participants, in order to be culturally responsive. For instance, Lee-Lin et al. (2012) reports how conducting focus groups in Mandarin and Cantonese was central to elicit cultural understandings of breast cancer and breast cancer screening from the Chinese women in their study. In other studies, having a moderator match the racial background of focus group participants was a strategy used to facilitate collaborative interactions among women participants (Thomas et al., 2014). However, as mentioned earlier, feminist-oriented focus groups can be led by facilitators who do not share the same cultural background as the focus group participants. This was the case in the study on women's lawbreaking, when Pollack (2003) a white woman, conducted a focus group with Black women prisoners.

Recruitment and Incentives. To recruit women for focus group participation, investigators commonly rely on their personal networks. Such sources of recruitment include community leaders, colleagues and friends (Madriz, 1998). For example, Pollack (2003) points out how her previous clients served as cultural guides, introducing her to other prisoners. In this way, Pollack was able to connect with more prisoners, which in turn, supported their willingness to participate in the focus group and disclose personal information about their experiences.

Other researchers report attending community events as a successful strategy when recruiting participants from diverse backgrounds. For example, Lee-Lin et al. (2012) recruited immigrants from China, Taiwan, Vietnam, and Hong Kong by attending various Chinese churches and Asian community centers (Lee-Lin et al., 2012). However, it should also be noted that other investigators identified difficulty accessing some women (e.g., Latina women) for their focus groups, especially if they are "recent immigrants or undocumented women, live on welfare, or engage in any nonnormative behavior such as alternative family living arrangements or working in the informal economy" (Madriz, 1998, p. 120). In these cases, incentives can be used to recruit women. However, incentives need to not only be attractive but also responsive to the needs of the women sought for the investigation. For instance, when recruiting Black graduate students for sista circles, Brown (2019) offered participants $25 gift cards as an incentive. Rather than decide where the gift cards would be purchased in advance, Brown (2019) allowed participants to decide where the gift card would come from. This strategy was responsive as graduate students, who typically have modest incomes, were given the opportunity to utilize the gift card in a way most beneficial to them. This recruiting strategy can also be viewed as somewhat empowering, as the sista circle participants were able to personalize their gift cards.

While economic incentives certainly have their place, they are not the only route to cultural responsiveness. In some cultures, women may not accept money for their focus group participation. As Madriz (1998) points out, "this an important aspect of Latina culture: Some women said that they felt uncomfortable receiving monetary compensation in exchange for *un favor a una amiga* [emphasis in original] [a favor to a friend]" (p. 120). As a result, Madriz (1998) offered her services as an educator in exchange for participation in the focus groups. These services involved conducting a presentation on violence against women to a class, taking a group of students on a college tour of an institution in which she taught, and participating in the graduation ceremony of student participants.

Ethical Considerations

In general, focus groups from a feminist-orientation aspire to maintain an ethical position that is committed to the well-being of others. Central to this ethical position is promoting supportive relationships among women and limiting further exploitation of or harm to women—particularly those from oppressed groups. However, the relational aspect of feminist-oriented focus groups does have unique ethical consequences. One ethical issue relates to how the intimacy established from feminist work can "move into a blurred space of friendship, sisterhood, and mentorship" (Bhattacharya, 2007, p. 1097). As a result of this blurred relationship, the participant may feel obligated as a friend to participate or continue participating in the focus group, despite any potential harm it may cause to her, her reputation or employment. In such cases, culturally responsive inquirers are cautioned to remind participants that they have the right to decline or discontinue their participation in a focus group session (McCormick, 2012).

It is also important to point out that the intimacy developed in the research relationship can also cause harm to investigators. For instance, investigators may feel emotionally burdened, wondering how ending the focus group research will impact their relationship with participants (McCormick, 2012). Planning how to responsibly end the researcher relationship *before* conducting feminist-oriented focus group research may help to reduce being emotionally overwhelmed by participants' feeling abandoned or betrayed when the research is completed. Also, investigators may find themselves intimately engaged with participants outside of the focus group research context, attending events with participants, sharing confidences or assisting participants with personal matters (i.e., providing relationship advice, locating housing) (Bhattacharya, 2007). Navigating these situations can give rise to a major ethical dilemma that involves trying to simultaneously uphold the social justice commitments of a feminist orientation and protecting one's self from harm (Bhattacharya, 2007; McCormick, 2012). Therefore, investigators must set clear boundaries with participants (McCormick, 2012) to reduce causing harm to themselves while aiming to advance social justice. In addition, thoroughly explaining the project to obtain informed consent is vital particularly when women have major concerns about participating in research because of their undocumented status (Madriz, 1998). Furthermore, other female populations require special considerations when being recruited for focus group research to ensure ethical and safe research practices. For example, before conducting her study with women prisoners, Pollack (2003) was required to have her project reviewed by a group of psychologists with the Correctional Service of Canada.

Summary

Feminism holds significant potential to disrupt deficit-based constructions of women, validate traditionally marginalized voices and produce knowledge about how women resist systematic oppression at the intersections of their cultural identities (i.e., race, gender, sexuality, ability). In recognition of the cultural diversity of women, various feminist orientations have emerged. Variant orientations of feminism acknowledge the unique cultural identities and experiences of women and treat these identities and experiences as sources of empowerment. Furthermore, a feminist orientation offers a way to explore how systematic oppression intersects with the social identities and experiences of women, and recast focus group methodology (i.e., sista circles) in ways that better align with the cultural particularities of participants. While different investigators use various feminist orientations and strategies to develop and implement focus groups, they share a commitment to center women, promote supportive relationships and avoid causing harm to women. Upholding these commitments reflects concern for the well-being of women. Yet, feminist-oriented focus groups are rife with unique complexities, including potentially harmful situations researchers encounter, while navigating relationships with participants. The case example Box 6.2 *Feminist-Intersectional Focus Groups* is a feminist-oriented focus group, informed by the notion of intersectionality, that discusses some ethical dilemmas and offers some strategies to navigate relationships with women participants.

Box 6.2 *Feminist-Intersectional Focus Groups*

Feminist-Intersectional Focus Groups

by Maureen A. Flint PhD, Stephanie Anne Shelton PhD,
and Kelly W. Guyotte, PhD

This project focused on women doctoral students' academic and social experiences in their academic programs. The setting for this study was a large public university in the southeastern United States, classified as "very-high research activity." Nineteen women enrolled in doctoral programs in the College of Education participated in the study.

Drawing from Crenshaw's (1989) concept of feminist intersectionality and Hill Collins' (1986) discussion of women as outsiders/insiders, we structured focus groups with the mindfulness that participants' experiences pursuing doctoral degrees included complexities beyond being women. The overarching methodology of the study incorporated qualitative methods in a focus group design (DeVault & Gross, 2014; Madriz, 2000). Participants were first invited to participate in individual interviews (~90 minutes), then invited to participate in small focus groups with approximately four participants each (~2 hours), and finally to participate in one of two large focus groups (~10 participants; ~2 hours).

The women who took part in the study varied widely in terms of parental, marital, employment, and student status (full-/part-time; first-generation-in-college; first-generation-indoctoral-studies; international student), as well as racial/ethnic identities, ages, socioeconomic backgrounds, and degree programs. For example, 6 of the 19 identified as women of color, 7 had children, and 7 were over 40-years-old.

Building from literature which described women doctoral students as experiencing alienation, isolation, and imposterism in their doctoral programs (e.g., Kurtz-Costes, Helmke, & Ulku-Steiner, 2006; Maher, Ford, & Thompson, 2004), we structured the research project to create space for sharing, validating, and appreciating participants' experiences.

During individual interviews, multiple women of color remarked on the pervasiveness of Whiteness on campus and in academia; women who had children described feeling isolated. Creating the focus groups, we scheduled participants with others who had expressed similar concerns and experiences, both to mitigate "outsider-ness," and to prevent tokenization and assumed responsibility for speaking either as a demographic representative or an anomaly. Following individual interviews, we met and discussed the women whom we had each interviewed, creating three intersectional groups. These groups centered (1) women who were married and/or had children; (2) women in their twenties; and (3) women who were working full-time. In creating these groupings, we were further mindful of women's intersectionality beyond these shared identities. For example, within each group we took into account each participant's age, race, marital status, and year in their program within each group, further extending connections and diversities beyond the shared elements on which we had based the groups. Though we did not announce our efforts to the participants, throughout small and large focus groups, the women oriented to their shared statuses, with statements such as, "I know y'all know what I'm talking about here when I say that juggling kids and a PhD is crazy."

Lessons Learned

During the small focus groups, the connections we hoped to engender between participants became relevant in both expected and unexpected ways. The conversations moved between discussions of balancing roles—mother/student/wife/staff member—as women affirmed one another's experiences and stories. An unexpected outcome that occurred following the small focus group was several participants' responses that they felt better about their experiences after participating. For example, one participant specifically noted in her small focus group that she was "so glad that I came..." noting that she had almost not attended. Reflections like this then informed our questioning during the large focus groups about the therapeutic qualities of qualitative research.

Beyond the opportunity for connection and affirmation, structuring the focus groups around shared identities also created spaces for disagreement and contradiction. For example, after one woman expressed her experiences feeling marginalized as a politically conservative woman within her doctoral studies, another student followed by sharing her experiences being similarly marginalized as an atheist, creating space for both students to respectfully empathize while also asserting perspectives contrary to the rest of the group (Shelton, Guyotte, & Flint, in press).

One major limitation was with time and coordination, particularly as we organized small focus groups based on women's shared experiences or identities. After receiving responses from the women regarding their availability, we had to shift our initial groupings into four smaller clusters. While these groupings had traces of our planned groups, we chose to prioritize including as many women as possible in the small focus groups, rather than maintaining our original intentions. We repeated this process as we sought to schedule the large focus group, ultimately deciding to hold two large focus groups. Other unexpected happenings affected our initial plans, such as only two participants attending one of the small focus groups. We negotiated these limitations while remaining mindful and thoughtful of our theoretical emphases on intersectionality.

Adjustments for future studies also include considerations regarding time. Our study was conducted over two academic semesters. This meant that some women's experiences in the study were stretched over several months, whereas others were condensed into a few weeks. Reflecting on this, we can see culturally responsive benefits and downsides of both; it would have been ideal to have had all participants on similar timelines in the study. An additional change would be lengthening the duration of the large focus groups. We had initially planned for each to last two hours, however, we easily exceeded our planned time. In the future, we might consider how to balance the desire to have more time with participants with consideration for the time that participants are giving up.

Related, throughout recruitment for the study, we discussed the tension between the times that we scheduled focus groups and individual interviews, and the women's busy lives. Specifically, as we scheduled focus groups and individual interviews, we discussed options for covering childcare for participants in the study. We asked women who might need childcare to reach out to us and had planned to explore resources for each request individually. Although ultimately none of the women requested childcare, future studies might consider how to provide this service for participants.

Ethical Considerations

A significant ethical consideration was our previous interactions with women in the study. All of the women who participated had taken classes with, worked alongside, or been advised by at least one of us. We were mindful of power dynamics and previous interactions in planning who facilitated interviews and focus groups. For example, we asked the women who they preferred as an interviewer and partnered researchers for small focus groups so that participants knew at least one of the facilitators.

As we considered how our questions privileged some voices and not others, or reflected on our own assumptions about women doctoral students' experiences, we were also attentive to the circulation of power throughout our facilitations. In particular, during small focus groups, some of the women critiqued their experiences in their programs or shared stories about particular faculty or courses they had taken. We were mindful of how Stephanie and Kelly's positions as faculty who had taught many of the women in the study might affect or inform participants' answers. One approach we took to mitigate this effect was for Maureen, a fellow student at the time, to ask the question, "What would you change about your programs?" while reiterating the confidentiality of the space.

Finally, reflecting our feminist underpinnings, we wondered what our roles were to respond, correct, or intervene in particular situations or moments. For example, during a small focus group Maureen and Stephanie facilitated, one of the women remarked, "I don't see color" and made several disparaging remarks about a class she had taken where the professor centered course materials around race. We wondered, both in the moment and afterward, what our role was to respond to these statements. Should we have intervened? Ultimately, both Stephanie and Maureen addressed the participant's comments indirectly in the follow-up questions they asked; however, the moment lingered with us as we considered facilitating future groups.

An overarching recommendation from our culturally responsive focus group practice is the importance of considering intersectionality. Had we created these groups on a single axis of identity, such as gender alone, we would have lost opportunities for connection, as well as moments of disagreement or difference. Reflecting on the large focus groups, in particular, these moments of difference became possible through the women's shared intersectional identities. In addition, our scaffolding from individual to larger focus groups meant that we could respond in culturally responsive ways in the midst of the narratives we heard.

Discussion Questions

1. How might you consider your positionalities when designing culturally responsive focus groups?

2. How do you attend to the nuances and complexities of your participants' experiences/identities?

References

Bhattacharya, K. (2007). Consenting to the consent form: What are the fixed and fluid understandings between the researcher and the researched? *Qualitative Inquiry, 13*(8), 1095–1115.

Brown, L. (2019). *"I've been conditioned to navigate": First-generation Black doctoral women and their persistence at a predominantly white institution.* [Unpublished doctoral dissertation]. University of Georgia, GA.

Carbado, D. W., Crenshaw, K. W., Mays, V. M., & Tomlinson, B. (2013). Intersectionality: Mapping the movements of a theory. *Du Bois review: social science research on race, 10*(2), 303–312.

Collier, J. (2017). *Using sista circles to examine sense of belonging of black women in doctoral programs at a historically white institution.* [Unpublished doctoral dissertation]. University of Georgia, GA.

Collins, P. (1986). Learning from the outsider within: The sociological significance of black feminist thought. *Social Problems, 33*(6), S14–S32.

Collins, P. H. (1990) *Black feminist thought: Knowledge, consciousness, and the politics of empowerment.* New York, NY: Routledge.

Cram, F. (2018). Conclusion: Lessons about Indigenous evaluation. In F. Cram, K. A. Tibbetts, & J. LaFrance (Eds.), (Special Issue) *Indigenous evaluation. New Directions for Evaluation, 159,* 121–133. San Francisco, CA: Jossey-Bass.

Crenshaw, K. (1989). Demarginalizing the intersection of race and sex: A black feminist critique of antidiscrimination doctrine, feminist theory and antiracist politics. *University of Chicago Legal Forum, 1*(8), 139–167.

Colucci, E. (2008). On the use of focus groups in cross-cultural research. In P. Liamputtong (Ed.), *Doing cross-cultural research.* (pp. 233–252). Dordrecht, Netherlands: Springer.

Danielsen, F., Jensen, P. M., Burgess, N. D., Coronado, I., Holt, S., Poulsen, M. K., Rueda, R. M., Skielboe, T., Enghoff, M., Hemmingsen, L. H., Sørensen, M., & Pirhofer-Walzl , K. (2014). Testing focus groups as a tool for connecting Indigenous and local knowledge on abundance of natural resources with science-based land management systems. *Conservation Letters, 7*(4), 380–389.

Dawson, A., Daniels, J., & Clapham, K. (2014). The contribution of focus group discussions to Aboriginal Australian health service research: A content analysis of practice and experience. *International Journal of Critical Indigenous Studies, 7*(2), 1–15.

DeVault, M. L., & Gross, G. (2014). Feminist qualitative interviewing: Experience, talk, and knowledge. In S. N. Hesse-Biber (Ed.), *Handbook of feminist research: Theory and praxis* (pp. 206–236). Thousand Oaks, CA: Sage.

Denzin, N. K., Lincoln, Y. S., & Smith, L. T. (Eds.). (2008). *Handbook of critical and indigenous methodologies.* Thousand Oaks, CA: Sage.

DiGiacomo, M., Delaney, P., Abbott, P., Davidson, P. M., Delaney, J., & Vincent, F. (2013). 'Doing the hard yards': Carer and provider focus group perspectives of accessing Aboriginal childhood disability services. *BMC health services research, 13*(1), 1–2.

Durie, M. (2011). Indigenizing mental health services: New Zealand experience. *Transcultural Psychiatry, 48*(1–2), 24–36.

Gorman, D., & Toombs, M. (2009). Matching research methodology with Australian indigenous culture. *Aboriginal and Islander Health Worker Journal, 33*(3), 4–7. Retrieved from http://eprints.usq.edu.au/id/eprint/5260

Halcomb, E. J., Gholizadeh, L., DiGiacomo, M., Phillips, J., & Davidson, P. M. (2007). Literature review: considerations in undertaking focus group research with culturally and linguistically diverse groups. *Journal of Clinical Nursing, 16*(6), 1000–1011.

Harding, S. (1991). *Whose science? whose knowledge? Thinking from women's lives.* Ithaca, NY: Cornell University Press.

Johnson, L. S. (2015). *Using sista circles to examine the professional experience of contemporary Black women teachers in schools: A collective story about school culture and support.* [Unpublished doctoral dissertation]. University of Georgia, Athens, GA.

Kariyawasam, K., & Guy, S. (2007). Intellectual property protection of Indigenous knowledge: Implementing initiatives at national and regional levels. *Deakin Law Review, 12*(2), 105–123. Retrieved from http://www.heinonline.org

Khupe, C., & Keane, M. (2017). Towards an African education research methodology: Decolonising new knowledge. *Educational Research for Social Change*, 6(1), 25–37.

Kovach, M. (2018). Doing Indigenous methodologies—a letter to a research class. In N. K. Denzin & Y. S. Lincoln (Eds.), *The Sage handbook of qualitative research* (5th ed., pp. 214–235). Los Angeles, CA: Sage.

Kurtz-Costes, B., Helmke, L. A., & Ulku-Steiner, B. (2006). Gender and doctoral studies: The perceptions of Ph.D. students in an American university. *Gender & Education, 18*(2), 137–155.

Lee-Lin, F., Menon, U., Nail, L., & Lutz, K. F. (2012). Findings from focus groups indicating what Chinese American immigrant women think about breast cancer and breast cancer screening. *Journal of Obstetric, Gynecologic & Neonatal Nursing, 41*(5), 627–637.

Madriz, E. I. (1998). Using focus groups with lower socioeconomic status Latina women. *Qualitative Inquiry, 4*(1), 114–128.

Maher, M. A., Ford, M. E., & Thompson, C. M. (2004). Degree progress of women doctoral students: Factors that constrain, facilitate, and differentiate. *Review of Higher Education, 27*(3), 385–408.

Martin, K. (2008). *Please knock before you enter: Aboriginal regulation of outsiders and the implications for researchers.* Teneriffe, Australia: Post Pressed.

McCormick, M. (2012). Feminist research ethics, informed consent, and potential harms. *The Hilltop Review, 6*(1), 5.

Mila-Schaaf, K., & Hudson, M. (2009b). *Negotiating space for indigenous theorising in Pacific mental health and addictions.* Auckland, NZ: Le Va.

Morgan, D. (2019). *Basic and advanced focus groups.* Thousand Oaks, CA: Sage.

National Congress of American Indians (2019). *Tribal nations and the United States: An introduction.* Retrieved from http://www.ncai.org/about-tribes

Neal-Barnett, A. M., Stadulis, R., Murray, M., Payne, M. R., Thomas, A., & Salley, B. B. (2011). Sister circles as a culturally relevant intervention for anxious Black women. *Clinical Psychology: Science and Practice, 18*(3), 266–273.

Ossai, N. B. (2010). African Indigenous knowledge systems (AIKS). *Simbiosis, 7*(2), 1–13.

Owusu-Ansah, F.E. & Mji, G. (2013). African indigenous knowledge and research. *African Journal of Disability, 2*(1), 1–5.

Parashar, S. (2016). Feminism and postcolonialism: (En) gendering encounters. *Postcolonial Studies*, 371–377.

Pere, L., & Barnes, A. (2009). New learnings from old understandings: Conducting qualitative research with Māori. *Qualitative Social Work, 8*(4), 449–467.

Peters, M. A., & Mika, C. T. (2017). Aborigine, Indian, Indigenous or First Nations? *Educational Philosophy and Theory, 49*(13), 1229–1234.

Pollack, S. (2003). Focus-group methodology in research with incarcerated women: Race, power, and collective experience. *Affilia, 18*(4), 461–472.

Prasad, P. (2017). *Crafting qualitative research* (2nd ed.). New York, NY: Routledge.

Romm, N. R. (2018). Reflections on a multi-layered intervention in the South African public education system: Some ethical implications for community operational research. *European Journal of Operational Research, 268*(3), 971–983.

Shelton, S.A., Guyotte, K.W., & Flint, M. (in press). Patchedworked (wo)monstros-
ities: Woman doctoral students cutting together/apart. *Reconceptualizing
Educational Research Methodology.*

Smith, L.T. (1999). *Decolonizing methodologies: Research and Indigenous peoples.*
London, UK: Zed Books.

Smith, G. (2000). Māori education: Revolution and transformative action. *Canadian Journal of Native Education,* 24(1), 57–72.

Smith, L. T. (2012). *Decolonizing methodologies: Research and Indigenous peoples.*
Dunedin, NZ: Otago University Press.

Tamasese, K., Peteru, C., Waldegrave, C., & Bush, A. (2005). Ole Taeao Afua, the
new morning: A qualitative investigation into Samoan perspectives on mental
health and culturally appropriate services. *Australian & New Zealand Journal of Psychiatry,* 39(4), 300–309.

Thomas, M., Vieten, C., Adler, N., Ammondson, I., Coleman-Phox, K., Epel, E.,
& Laraia, B. (2014). Potential for a stress reduction intervention to promote
healthy gestational weight gain: Focus groups with low-income pregnant
women. *Women's Health Issues,* 24(3), e305–e311.

Waapalaneexkweew (Bowman, N., Mohican/Lunaape), & Dodge-Francis, C.
(2018). Culturally responsive Indigenous evaluation and tribal governments:
Understanding the relationship. In F. Cram, K. A. Tibbetts, & J. LaFrance
(Eds.), (Special Issue) *Indigenous evaluation. New Directions for Evaluation,*
159, 17–31. San Francisco, CA: Jossey-Bass.

Wilkinson, S. (1999). Focus groups: A feminist method. *Psychology of Women
Quarterly,* 23(2), 221–244.

United Nations. (2019). *Indigenous peoples at the UN.* Department of Economic
and Social Affairs: Indigenous Peoples. Retrieved from https://www.un.org/
development/desa/indigenouspeoples/about-us.html

CHAPTER SEVEN

Culturally Responsive Online Focus Groups

In This Chapter

- Online Focus Groups: A Brief Overview

- Technology Considerations

- Online Focus Group Questions, Environment, Size, and Participation

- Moderating Online Focus Groups

- Online Focus Group Recruitment and Incentives

- Ethical Considerations in Conducting Online Focus Groups

- A Case Example: Using Black Feminist Thought to Conduct Online Focus Groups with Black Mothers

TECHNOLOGICAL IMPROVEMENTS IN ONLINE communication have led to the emergence of online focus groups (Fielding, Lee, & Blank, 2017). As a result, studies including online focus groups with different populations in health and social science research, for example, have increased in recent years (Liamputtong, 2011). Yet, despite their popularity, there is disagreement as to whether online, or "virtual" focus groups, facilitate an interactive dialogue among participants—a distinct benefit of traditional focus groups (Bloor et al., 2001; Murgado-Armenteros et al., 2012). In response to such disagreements, some researchers contend, "if we accept that the interactions of cyberspace are social, the most accurate or 'naturalistic' recreation of these interactions for a focus group discussion would be using this medium" (Bloor et al. 2001, p. 78). In agreement with those that recognize the online context as a social space able to produce interactive focus group discussions, I not only suggest that the use of online focus groups is indeed a legitimate way to collect focus group data (Bloor et al., 2001; Douglas, Hines, Dixon, Celi, & Lysova, 2018) but also a tool with powerful potential to elicit insights from some of the most hard-to-reach and vulnerable cultural groups.

With this perspective on online focus groups in mind, this chapter provides an overview of online focus groups, focusing on synchronous (real-time) and asynchronous (not real-time). The advantages and disadvantages of both types of online focus groups are discussed. General suggestions and recommendations are offered related to online technology as well as online focus group size, recruitment and incentives, participation, questions, moderating and environment. Empirical examples of how online focus groups were used with hard-to-reach and vulnerable or marginalized groups are woven throughout the chapter. To provide further guidance on how to use online focus groups responsively, and ethical considerations when conducting online focus groups, a case example demonstrating the use of a videoconferencing platform to conduct online focus groups with Black mothers who use Facebook for breastfeeding support is presented.

Online Focus Groups: A Brief Overview

Focus groups conducted online can vastly extend the geographic reach of a study by providing access for participants who are dispersed or in remote settings (Krueger & Casey, 2009; Reid & Reid, 2005). Online focus groups may also provide greater convenience for participants, reducing the need for travel (Smith et al., 2009). Moreover, online focus groups are cost-effective, eliminating facility rental costs (Hennink, 2014). Furthermore, online focus groups have been used in responsive ways with hard-to-research and vulnerable populations that include, but are not limited to transgender women (Reisner et al., 2017), male victims of intimate partner violence (Douglas, Hines, Dixon, Celi, & Lyvosa, 2018), LGBTQ+ (lesbian, gay, bisexual, transgender, queer/questioning, and others) young adults (Ramo, Meacham, Thrul, Belohlavek, Sarkar, & Humfleet, 2019), individuals who use wheeled mobility devices (i.e., manual and power wheelchairs) (Ripat & Colatruglio, 2016), and Black breastfeeding mothers (Robinson, Davis, Hall, Lauckner, & Anderson, 2019). Online focus groups, however, rely on participants having access to the Internet, which may present a barrier for participation. As a result of some cultural groups' not having access to the Internet, some online focus groups may reflect the views of people who tend to have more education or higher incomes (Abrams & Gaiser, 2017). Notwithstanding, populations who have access to the Internet are still valuable sources, reflecting a good amount of within-group cultural diversity (Abrams & Gaiser, 2017).

Two types of online focus groups are commonly used by qualitative researchers and evaluators: synchronous or asynchronous online focus groups (Hennink, 2014). The following sections describe synchronous and asynchronous online focus groups, highlighting some of their features, strengths and limitations.

Synchronous online focus groups. Synchronous online focus groups are like traditional focus group sessions as they are conducted in real time, giving them a similar dynamic of a live discussion. One form of synchronous online focus groups is text-based focus groups. Hennink (2014) notes that text-based focus groups are beneficial for "youth who are very comfortable using technology-based communications, those with mobility restrictions hampering their physical attendance at a face-to-face focus group, or those with concerns about attending a face-to-face group" (p. 9). In text-based focus group discussions, participants do not see or hear each other; they establish their interaction through typing. Lobe (2017) indicates that "the typical online venue for this type of online focus group are various instant messaging applications (Audium, MSN, AIM, Google Hangouts, etc.) and Web Messaging facilities (e.g. Facebook Live Messenger, Jive Chime, etc.)" (p. 230). Such messaging applications involve a high degree of interaction as participants can respond to messages as soon as they are made available on their computer (Chen & Hinton, 1999).

However, text-based focus group participation is significantly influenced by participants' ability to type. For instance, those who type faster have the potential to dominate the discussion (Mann & Stewart, 2000) and those who have discomfort with typing or low literacy levels may be limited in sharing their viewpoints (Wirtz, Cooney, Chaudhry, & Reisner, 2019).

In considering the possible advantage of those who type faster, Lobe (2008) suggests that the optimal number of participants in text-based online focus groups range from three to four, so as not to allow the faster typists to dominate the conversation. Also, more brief and superficial answers may result from text-based online focus groups. Therefore, text-based online focus group facilitation requires an experienced moderator who can stimulate participants' engagement with each other, rather than merely respond to the questions posed by the moderator (Short, 2006). Furthermore, in text-based online discussions, transcriptions are generated as participants type their responses, eliminating (or reducing) transcription costs (Walston & Lissitz, 2000). However, transcriptions generated from online focus groups do not conform to standard transcription conventions discussed in Chapter 8.

Text-based online focus groups offer anonymity as participants do not see each other. Yet this anonymity can be compromised if participants have previous relationships with each other or are part of a preexisting group (Krueger & Casey, 2015). Furthermore, information from nonverbal signs, which contributes great richness to the analysis of the discourse, is not captured in text- and audio-based synchronous online focus groups. This increases the likelihood of misunderstandings between participants and may also obscure nuances in meaning critical to interpretation (Reisner et al., 2018). However, text-based users can use emotional icons or emoticons to express their emotions. Emoticons are a common way to express emotions for most people when online and can compensate for the loss of rich nonverbal layers of communication that characterizes text-based interactions (Liamputtong, 2011). Another form of synchronous online focus group involves the use of videoconferencing platform. This focus group platform has become popular with the ubiquity of webcams in computers, laptops and other devices such as smartphones and notebooks (Abrams et al., 2015). This form of online focus group offers text-based and audio as well as video functions. The use of this technology allows researchers to capture some nonverbal communications and easily record online focus group sessions.

Videoconferencing platforms are useful to access and engage hard-to-reach populations and facilitate geographical diversity. For example, one study used a videoconferencing platform to conduct online focus groups with male victims of partner abuse—a hard-to-reach population, as they are often denied or turned away when they seek support or services (Douglas,

Hines, Dixon, Celi, & Lyvosa, 2018). The study was designed to examine the experiences of male victims of partner abuse across international contexts and included 41 men from Australia, Canada, England, and the United States. A total of 12 focus groups (three in each country) were conducted (Douglas et al., 2018). The researchers report how

> finding enough men in one geographic region who have sought help, to conduct multiple focus groups, is not feasible as it is when studying female victims. Thus, this technology [synchronous online focus groups] allowed us to bring together a geographically diverse group of victims and participants. (p. 14).

Synchronous online focus group platforms also give participants the ability to log in using a pseudonym, opt-out of questions, and easily remove themselves from the focus group discussion by muting the audio or turning off the video (webcam) feature. These aspects of synchronous online focus groups maintain participant confidentiality and allow participants to control their level of participation (Douglas et al., 2018; Wirtz et al., 2019). In addition, the geographic distance between participants and the ability of participants to join the group from a remote and private location helps participants to feel more comfortable disclosing information. These aspects of videoconferencing platforms are advantageous when collecting sensitive information from marginalized groups (Douglas et al., 2018; Wirtz, Cooney, Chaudhry, & Reisner, 2019).

As when conducting face-to-face focus groups, researchers using synchronous online focus groups may face challenges. One challenge concerns participant turn-taking during the focus group discussion. Turn-taking issues commonly involve overlap in talk (Wirtz et al., 2019). Yet, this issue is considered a minor problem as participants typically recognize when they were talking over someone and eventually allow each other to take turns speaking (Wirtz et al., 2019). Differences in audio and Internet connection quality present another challenge with using synchronous, online focus groups. In most cases, audio quality issues can be resolved by simply letting participants know when they cannot be heard or having participants keep their audio (and sometimes video) feature turned off when they are not speaking (Wirtz et al., 2019). In terms of Internet connectivity issues, researchers will need to be able to troubleshoot issues with the technology as they arise. In my own experience with online focus groups, the note taker was responsible for troubleshooting, leaving me with the flexibility to fully focus on moderating the online focus group. Also, I have found asking participants to log in a few minutes early provides an opportunity to resolve technology issues before the focus group begins. See Table 7.1 *Synchronous Online Focus Groups*, for a summary of the advantages and disadvantages of synchronous focus groups.

Table 7.1: *Synchronous Online Focus Groups*

Advantages of Synchronous Focus Groups	Disadvantages of Synchronous Focus Groups
• A higher degree of responsiveness and interactivity • Possible access to geographically remote participants • Ease of transcribing (text-based) and recording of discussions with online tools	• Relies on the technological ability of participants • Requires highly experienced moderators to deepen the discussions • Relies on participants' internet quality • Unable to interpret many non-verbal signs during the discussion (text-based) • Unable to collect non-verbal information during the discussion • Hard to manage turn-taking in discussions

Asynchronous online focus groups. Asynchronous online focus groups, also known as bulletin board focus groups, consist of a series of postings, beginning with a question posed by the moderator and followed by contributions from participants (Hennink, 2014; Krueger & Casey, 2015; Stewart & Shamdasani, 2015). The bulletin board format is text-based and allows focus group members to see and respond to the comments made by others. Whereas participants using a videoconferencing platform log in at a particular time, participants in asynchronous focus groups can respond to comments posted on the bulletin board at any time of the day or night (Stewart

& Shamdasani, 2015). Because participants can respond at their convenience and have more time to process and compose their responses, the asynchronous focus group format tends to generate more thoughtful discussions and detailed responses as compared to a face-to-face focus group discussion (Bloor et al., 2001; Krueger & Casey, 2015; Stewart & Shamdasani, 2015). However, bulletin board focus group participants have a limited time span within which to participate in the online focus group (Krueger & Casey, 2015). For example, one study hosted an online asynchronous focus group for seven days to understand environmental barriers to community participation in cold weather climates among wheelchair users (Ripat & Colatruglio, 2016). Eight individuals who use wheeled mobility devices (manual and power wheelchairs, scooters, etc.) participated in the online focus group (Ripat & Colatruglio, 2016). The moderator posted questions each day, and participants were asked to respond to the moderator's questions and each others' comments. As a result of participants engaging in the focus group for seven consecutive days and having time to reflect on their responses, the researchers contend the asynchronous focus group "yielded rich and thoughtful data" (Ripat & Colatruglio, 2016).

Bulletin board focus groups facilitate discussion with populations less likely to participate in face-to-face focus groups, and offer privacy (Krueger & Casey, 2015; Reisner et al., 2018). For instance, one study used secret Facebook groups (i.e., a private group, undetectable to the public) to conduct asynchronous focus groups with caregivers of children with sensory processing disorder (SPD) for about two months. The therapeutic needs of the children with SPD often restrict their caregivers' availability to conduct in-person focus groups. Therefore, using the Facebook secret group format was considered ideal to meet caregivers' convenience needs and protect their privacy (Medley-Rath, 2019). Moreover, many Americans, including caregivers, are familiar with and use social media for support (Medley-Rath, 2019). Using the Facebook secret group format, then, resembled how caregivers already use social media in their daily lives (Medley-Rath, 2019).

Over the course of an asynchronous online focus group, a moderator has more time to share new questions, post comments in response to participants' posts and encourage participants to respond to the comments of others (Stewart & Shamdasani, 2015). Furthermore, an asynchronous focus group gives moderators opportunities to deal with concerns, or address participants who are not posting comments on the bulletin board using private messaging features (Bloor et al., 2001). Asynchronous online focus groups also allow a sense of anonymity, which can lead to enhanced honesty and disclosure. For instance, in a study that used asynchronous online focus groups to explore breastfeeding mothers' use of social media, participants were asked to reflect on their experiences participating in a secret Facebook online focus group. Participants reported that they felt "very comfortable sharing honest information, and to a higher degree than they would in a face-to-face focus group" (Skelton et al., 2018, p. 6). In another study using asynchronous online focus groups to explore sexual health care access with 29 female-to-male transgender adults in the United States, the format was found particularly advantageous to discuss sensitive health topics (Reisner et al., 2018). Yet, asynchronous forms have some limitations. Like text-based synchronous online focus groups, asynchronous platforms are unable to capture information from nonverbal cues. However, as mentioned earlier, nowadays people use emoticons, which can help to convey feelings. Table 7.2, *Asynchronous Online Focus Groups*, provide an overview of the advantages and disadvantages of asynchronous focus groups.

In the following sections, I offer some general suggestions and recommendations related to online focus groups.

Table 7.2: *Asynchronous Online Focus Groups*

Advantages of Asynchronous Focus Groups	Disadvantages of Asynchronous Focus Groups
• Ability to recruit participants from different time zones	• Risk of shorter contributions than in face-to-face groups
• Cost and time effectiveness through having an immediately written transcript of the discussion	• Reduced continuity and flow of communication
• More time for participants to reflect before responding	• Requiring 24 hours of moderation
• Ease of moderation by having more time to engage the discussions and reassure reluctant participants	• Inability to capture information from nonverbal signs
• Enhanced participant honesty and disclosure of sensitive information	

Technology Considerations

When designing an online focus group study, culturally responsive inquirers will need to decide on the type of online format most appropriate for the population they are seeking to engage. Reisner et al. (2017) and Krueger and Casey (2015) offer some recommendations worthy of consideration when deciding what type of technology to use:

- Consult with technology-savvy individuals to understand the platforms best suited to work with potential participants and supported by your environment.

- Resist the desire to incorporate unnecessary technology as these extra features may potentially confuse participants.

- Select technology that participants may already be comfortable using, in order to maximize the potential of the online focus group and generate rich information.

- Decide if the technology will enhance participation and or encourage disclosure of sensitive information.

- Consider the possible trade-offs regarding the spontaneity and thoughtfulness that can occur between the moderator and participants.

- Keep the technology itself in the background. This means interactions with the technology should not dominate the focus group. Rather, participants' conversation and interactions should be the stars of the show.

- Practice using the technology to understand its functions and identify features that need modifications or specific instructions for participants.

Furthermore, when considering the use of online focus groups for an investigation, culturally responsive inquirers need to be aware that the use of technology can exclude certain groups who do not have access to reliable Internet from participating. In the context of the United States, this often includes people who are elderly, less educated, or members of communities of color (Douglas et al., 2018).

Online Focus Group Questions

Stewart and Shamdasani (2015) recommend giving online focus groups 12 to 15 questions, depending on the topic covered. As in face-to-face focus group protocols, online focus group questions should be targeted and organized, including transitions from one topic to the next. Beginning the online focus group discussions with questions that allow participants to introduce themselves encourages group cohesion (Reisner et al., 2017). Another strategy involves the use of follow-up questions to stimulate rich responses and interactions throughout the discussion (Reisner et al., 2017). When developing questions for a bulletin board focus groups, you will want to decide on the topics to cover each day. Ripat and Colatrugio (2016) provided topics and questions for several days for their bulletin board focus groups examining environmental barriers to community participation in cold weather climates among wheelchair users. The topics for each day included: introductions (day 1); wheeled mobility and community participation/facilitators/challenges (days 2/3/4); solutions to participation challenges (day 5); how to implement change (day 6); and reflection/additional comments (day 7). See Ripat and Colatrugio (2016, p. 98) for specific questions asked each day.

Online Focus Group Environment

Participants will have a more enjoyable experience, leading to more interaction, if they feel the environment is attractive and easy to navigate. Therefore, the appearance of the online focus group venue matters. Kruger and Casey (2015) identify some ways to enhance the online focus group environment:

- *Make it welcoming*: Consider how the environment appears to participants. Would participants find the environment inviting? Would a picture or a cover photo make the page (i.e., Facebook) more aesthetically appealing? Would a video introducing yourself and welcoming participants be appropriate? Is the environment user-friendly? Does the site contain the information necessary to conduct the online focus groups? Are special instructions necessary?

- *Personalize it*: As appropriate, allow the participants the opportunity to personalize the environment. For example, depending on the online environment, participants can pick an avatar, use an alias, or identify themselves creatively (by a type of flower, or breed of dog).

- *Keep layout and design simple*: Be sure the site is visually stimulating but not cluttered, and make things on the site easy for participants to locate.

Online Focus Group Size

The number of participants in the synchronous text- or video-based online focus groups is typically somewhat smaller than face-to-face or asynchronous groups in practice. This is for two reasons. First, it is more difficult to keep track of the other participants when they cannot be seen. Second, even when visual contact is available through online video groups, a large group is not recommended because the section of the screen showing other participants can get crowded for those who do not have large monitors. Hence, the recommended size for synchronous online focus groups would be considered around four to six participants (Lobe, 2017); the consensus is that an online focus group should last for about an hour (Poynter, 2010).

In terms of asynchronous online focus groups, the group size can be larger, as moderators do not have to manage participants in real time. Further, as previously mentioned, because moderators can host a focus group over consecutive days (Ripat & Colatruglio, 2016), or months (Medley-Rath, 2019), this format allows moderators time to provide more reflective and individual responses to participants, in much the same way a moderator would do in a face-to-face focus group. While there is no consensus on focus group size for asynchronous online focus groups, they typically have from 10 to 30 participants (Poytner, 2010).

Online Focus Group Participation

In an online focus group, it is good to establish ground rules right away. In synchronous online focus groups, the moderator may establish explicit guidelines for turn-taking during the conversation. In asynchronous online focus groups, they may need to provide clear guidance regarding when and how participants are expected to post their responses. For example, in the study of caregivers of children with SPD, the researcher gave explicit instructions to the online participants in the secret Facebook group. Each participant was asked to "visit the group twice a day and spend 15-30 minutes each day answering new questions and interacting with other participants in the forum" (Medley-Ruth, 2019, p. 1770). Participation in online focus groups can also be enhanced by activities. In bulletin board online format, for example, the moderator could assign a task related to the topic and ask participants to post their results the next day (Krueger & Casey, 2015). Incorporating storytelling into the online focus group is another technique used to stir participation. For instance, in a study utilizing bulletin board online focus groups to examine how transgender persons access sexual healthcare services, researchers provided the following prompt to elicit stories:

> *If you feel comfortable, please share a story about a recent inter-action you had with a health care provider that demonstrates how your gender identity affects interaction with a provider.* (Reisner et al., 2017, p. 1668)

Requesting stories from participants during asynchronous online focus groups generated detailed narratives rather than short or single-word responses (Reisner et al., 2017). Participation in online focus groups can also be enhanced by using a platform that provides multiple options (i.e., smartphone, app, notebook) for participants to access the focus group discussion (Wirtz et al., 2019).

Moderating Online Focus Groups

Stewart and Williams (2005) found that discussions in online focus groups can be more complex. Therefore, moderating them requires unique skills. For example, while participating in an online focus group conducted via a videoconferencing platform, participants may become distracted by something (i.e., email) in their environment. Therefore, moderators who encounter an inattentive participant will need to be able to gracefully veer the participant's attention back to the discussion (Douglas et al., 2018). Other general recommendations for moderating online focus groups include: being attentive to group dynamics and silences that occur (in video online groups) (Liamputtong, 2011); having two facilitators (one to guide the focus and one to assist with troubleshooting and participant questions that might arise) (Krueger & Casey, 2015); remaining available to receive backchannel/private communications from participants (Reisner et al., 2017); and making adjustments to the protocol to avoid participant drop-out or fatigue (Reisner et al., 2017).

Online Focus Group Recruitment and Incentives

Many of the same recruitment tactics as those used in face-to-face focus group (i.e., flyers, announcements) can be used to identify participants for online focus groups (Stewart & Shamdasani, 2015). Depending on the study and target cultural group, it may be appropriate to send virtual study announcements or invitations to potential participants. To recruit caregivers of children with SPD online focus groups using a secret Facebook group function, for example, Medley-Rath (2019) used a combination of recruitment methods. She asked people in her personal networks to share flyers. Medley-Rath (2019) also shared her study on her social media accounts, and asked authors of books about SPD, and administrators of social media groups, to share her flyer on their websites.

Like face-to-face focus groups, recruitment for online focus groups can include monetary incentives (i.e., gift cards). Financial incentives may be especially attractive to participants who are being asked to participate in bulletin board online focus groups for an extended period (Krueger & Casey, 2015). Yet, as Krueger and Casey (2015) point out, intangible incentives for participating in focus groups often go unnoticed. For example, the benefits of the knowledge gained by listening to other online focus group participants with similar backgrounds or interests may not be obvious to participants. Therefore, it is recommended that any potential benefit from participating in online focus groups are communicated to participants (Krueger & Casey, 2015). Notwithstanding, incentives cannot guarantee that participants will not leave an online group (Stewart & Shamdasani, 2015). This is particularly the case for asynchronous online focus groups that last over several days or months. There are several reasons for participant attrition. Health issues, travel, and loss of interest are just some reasons. In other cases, people may agree to participate in the online focus group but fail to register, or they register but do not show up (Stewart & Shamdasani, 2015). To limit online focus group attrition, make clear when the online focus group will occur and the time commitment involved (Stewart & Shamdasani, 2015).

Online Ethical Considerations

Many ethical considerations for face-to-face focus groups also apply to online focus groups. However, implementing ethical practices in online settings poses a distinct challenge. In the online context, ensuring participants have thoroughly read and fully understood the consent information is more difficult. It is helpful to provide project and consent information in ways that are accessible and succinct. For example, when using a videoconferencing online format, a PowerPoint shared from the moderator's screen, or in the case of a web-based format (i.e., Facebook) an initial page with the study and consent information presented concisely is useful. Emailing a link to an online consent form containing study information is also beneficial (Reisner et al., 2017). Another key ethical concern when conducting focus groups online is ensuring participant safety. This is especially the case when working with stigmatized or vulnerable populations. In their study using a videoconferencing platform to investigate male victims of partner violence, Douglas et al. (2018) included a recruitment statement in clear language with red lettering to ensure the protection of potential participants:

> *Please note! If you are currently in an abusive relationship, you should think very carefully about whether your participation in this project can be carried out safely. For example, will your partner be able to read your emails to us and from us? Will your partner be aware of you participating in the online discussion group? Remember, unless a website has been set up in a specific way, people can trace your history on the computer—that is they can see what sites you have been logged onto. They will be able to trace that you have accessed the weblink to our online group unless you know how to effectively delete this history. Think—would taking part threaten your safety in any way? Please do not take any further part in this study if it does.* (p. 10)

Other general strategies for maintaining safety and confidentiality when conducting focus groups online, according to Douglas et al. (2018), include (1) assigning pseudonyms for participants to use when they log in, (2) encouraging participants to use or create an email address that does not include their name, and (3) instructing participants to conduct the online focus group in a private location.

Some online focus group platforms generate additional privacy issues. For example, Medley-Rath (2019) points out if Facebook is used for the online focus group but the participant does not log out of Facebook, or have a password-protected phone, the focus group could be joined by anyone who has access to the device (computer, phone). To mitigate this issue, Medley-Rath, (2019) suggests participants can review their Facebook privacy settings, activate a two-step authentication process, or protect their device (computer, notebook, mobile phone) using passwords. Confirming participants' eligibility to give consent and making sure they are not underage can also be a concern when conducting online focus groups. Reisner et al. (2017) suggest that screening potential participants by telephone can help to lessen this concern as "eligibility can be more confidently assessed during a phone conversation than via email or online" (p. 1663).

Summary

While researchers have questioned the legitimacy of online focus groups, the empirical research presented in this chapter demonstrates the potential of online focus groups to be uniquely responsive to marginalized groups. Specifically, the online investigations discussed in this chapter show how important it is to offer participants a safe environment. This will encourage them, especially those in vulnerable or marginalized groups, to disclose potentially sensitive information. Furthermore, online focus groups were found by researchers to extend the geographical reach of their research, providing remote access to hard-to-reach populations. That said, culturally responsive inquirers will need to carefully examine the features of online formats (synchronous, asynchronous) to determine the extent to which a platform is appropriate for a certain cultural group, and the social justice aims of the project. Overall, when carefully implemented, online focus groups can be culturally responsive given their capacity to provide social spaces for diverse participants to interact in comfortable and meaningful ways. The following case example outlined in Box 7.1, *Using Black Feminist Thought to Conduct Online Focus Groups with Black Mothers*, illustrates how a videoconferencing platform was used to facilitate online focus groups. This example highlights the geographical diversity enabled by the online focus group format, as well as drawing attention to the roles of the moderator, theory, and the note taker to facilitate cultural responsiveness, privacy, and technology.

Box 7.1 *Using Black Feminist Thought to Conduct Online Focus Groups with Black Mothers*

Using Black Feminist Thought to Conduct Online Focus Groups with Black Mothers

by Ayanna Robinson, MPH, PhD

A variety of factors contribute to breastfeeding disparities and early breastfeeding cessation. Support for breastfeeding, for example, is a strong predictor of breastfeeding outcomes, including the extent to which a mother will achieve her own breastfeeding goals (McFadden et al., 2017; Centers for Disease Control and Prevention, 2013). Support for breastfeeding mothers can be provided in person, by phone, and also online, like through social media, yet less is known about the exchange of breastfeeding support online (McFadden et al., 2017). According to a study by the Pew Research Center, the majority of mothers who report using social media also report exchanging social support within these settings (Duggan, Lenhart, Lampe, & Ellison, 2015). At the time when I conducted this study, few studies explored the use of social media among mothers to exchange breastfeeding support, however (Bridges, 2016; Asiodu, Waters, Dailey, Lee, & Lyndon, 2015). The purpose of this study was to explore how African American mothers experience breastfeeding support on Facebook, and associations with breastfeeding outcomes.

The study was situated within the field of public health, where increasing breastfeeding rates is a Healthy People 2020 goal (United States Breastfeeding Committee, 2014). The setting was Facebook communities for breastfeeding support. Participants were recruited from six mom-to-mom support groups for Black mothers, five of which were specifically dedicated to providing breastfeeding support. Three of the five breastfeeding support groups targeted mothers in specific geographic locations in the United States. Two groups had national representation, while the other three groups targeted mothers in specific states. The number of group members at the time of data collection ranged from 104 to 26,000 members (Robinson et al., 2019).

Black feminist thought provided the primary lens and culturally responsive approach for the study design, including data collection and analysis. The epistemology of Black feminist thought involves assessing truths that are widely accepted among Black women. These truths are based on the collective lived experiences and worldviews of Black women, which have been sustained throughout the history of Black women in American society (Collins, 2000). Black feminist thought, therefore, provided a framework to present the unique perspectives of African American women and center their experiences as the criteria of meaning. It also allowed me to explore concepts like intersectionality and self-identity among the lived experiences of Black mothers who participate in breastfeeding support groups on Facebook.

I conducted a sequential mixed-methods research study. During phase 1 of data collection, I collected survey data from 277 mothers who participated in Facebook breastfeeding support groups. The survey measured breastfeeding support received on Facebook and from other sources; it also looked at breastfeeding attitudes, self-efficacy, perceived norms, current duration and intended duration of breastfeeding. During phase 2, I conducted focus groups and a qualitative content analysis exploring the types of support mothers exchanged within their Facebook support group. The methodological decision to conduct focus groups in feminist research, and in this study, reinforces the value placed on honoring the voices of participants. Use of focus groups may also balance the power differences between the participants and the researcher (Johnson-Bailey, 2004; Patton, 2015).

Focus group participants (N=22) were a subset of participants who completed the Phase 1 survey. Participants self-identified as first-time, African American mothers, and were breastfeeding at the time of data collection. All participants were at least 18 years old and participants' ages ranged from 22 to 40, with the average of 30 years. In recruiting participants for the focus groups, I used stratified sampling methods to represent the diverse population of mothers who participated in the Facebook support groups. Participants represented a range of geographic locations, household incomes, ages, and educational backgrounds. Black feminist thought underscores the importance of highlighting diversity, rather than perpetuating the homogeneity of Black women. It is therefore critical to conduct research that includes a cross-section of African American women.

I conducted four, 90-minute synchronous focus groups online using the videoconferencing platform, Zoom. Before conducting the focus groups, the focus group guide was pre-tested among a group of African American mothers, and reviewed by other breastfeeding researchers. The questions in the guide explored the constructs measured in the survey and the experiences of mothers in their Facebook support groups. There were five to six participants in each group. Participants used an ID and password to access the online meeting rooms and participated using their webcams or cellular phones. Member checking was an imperative step in enhancing the credibility of my findings, promoting cultural competency, and centering the voices of the participants. After each focus group, I verbally summarized my notes for participants and invited them to provide feedback and additional comments. Focus groups were video and audio recorded, and a professional transcription company transcribed the audio recordings. I analyzed the data both inductively and deductively, using thematic analysis and coded aspects of Black feminist thought, including counter-narratives, social activism, empowerment and resistance, as appropriate (Robinson et al., 2019). Another African American researcher and subject matter expert reviewed and critiqued the codes and themes I created. In a final round of member checking, I invited focus group participants to review the draft manuscript and provide feedback. In conducting these member checks, I created a cyclical process of open communication and transparency between myself and the research participants.

There were three themes and two subthemes, which are published in an article by Robinson et al. (2019). The overarching themes included creating a community for Black mothers, online interactions and levels of engagement, and empowerment of self and others.

Lessons Learned

There were several strengths in the focus group approach used in this study. Foremost, as the focus group moderator, being the same gender and race as my focus group participants created a foundation for developing trust and dialogue as participants shared on a sensitive and vulnerable topic in motherhood (Johnson-Bailey, 2004). I was also assisted by a note taker, who was also an African American woman. It was apparent that, as both a Black woman and a mother, I was viewed as an insider by participants. I was also assisted by a note taker, who was also an African American woman. Our shared identities were another methodological decision to enhance the cultural competency of the research design, afforded a layer of trust. Using an online platform to conduct the focus groups also fostered participant autonomy by providing the flexibility to join from a convenient location, e.g., at home as they nursed their children, which was less disruptive to their lives as new mothers.

Conducting focus groups online is not without limitations, however. Online focus groups require skilled moderation to maintain rapport and participant engagement and to balance focus group dynamics in an online setting. Nonverbal cues are also lost when participants do not use video cameras. Although most participants used webcams or mobile video cameras, engaging participants who participated without video use required more thoughtfulness and awareness. I recommend the use of video cameras when conducting online focus groups, if possible.

Maintaining the confidentiality and privacy of the participants is an important ethical consideration for conducting online focus groups. Using audio versus video recordings for transcriptions, and creating password protected meeting rooms are ways to protect the confidentiality of the participants. Finally, in addition to taking notes, the notetaker played an invaluable role in assisting with the logistics of the online focus groups, such as troubleshooting technical difficulties experienced by participants and responding to questions posted in the discussion box. The technical assistance allowed the focus groups to proceed with minimal interruptions. When conducting online focus groups, I also recommend having a note taker, or another individual present who can assist with logistics, as needed.

Online focus groups provide qualitative researchers with an opportunity to connect with populations across geographic locations and can minimize barriers to participate in research due to time constraints or location barriers. By conducting an online focus group with mothers, many of whom were within the first six months postpartum, and all of whom were nursing, I provided a convenient way for participants to share their experiences with receiving online support. Also, Black feminist thought provided a framework to explore the intersections of race, class, and gender as well as sociocultural and historical factors that impact the lived experiences and health outcomes of the Black women in my study.

Discussion Questions

1. What are the circumstances in which conducting online focus groups may be more advantageous than conducting in-person focus groups? What are the circumstances in which conducting in-person focus groups may be more advantageous? Why?

2. What techniques can researchers use to maintain participant engagement when conducting focus groups online?

References

Abrams, K. M., Wang, Z., Song, Y. J., & Galindo-Gonzalez, S. (2015). Data richness trade-offs between face-to-face, online audiovisual, and online text-only focus groups. *Social Science Computer Review, 33*(1), 80–96.

Bloor, M., Frankland, J., Thomas, M., and Robson, K. (2001). *Focus Groups in Social Research*. London, UK: Sage.

Bridges, N. (2016). The faces of breastfeeding support: Experiences of mothers seeking breastfeeding support online. *Breastfeeding Review: Professional Publication of the Nursing Mothers' Association of Australia, 24*(1), 11–20.

Chen, P., & Hinton, S. M. (1999). Realtime interviewing using the world wide web. *Sociological Research Online, 4*(3), 1–19.

Collins, P. H. (2000). *Black feminist thought: Knowledge, consciousness, and the politics of empowerment* (2nd ed.). New York: Routledge.

Douglas, E. M., Hines, D. A., Dixon, L., Celi, E. M., & Lysova, A. V. (2018). Using technology to conduct focus groups with a hard-to-reach population: A methodological approach concerning male victims of partner abuse in four English-speaking countries. *Journal of Interpersonal Violence*, 1–19.

Duggan. M., Lenhart, A., Lampe, C., & Ellison, N. (2015). *Parents and social media: Mothers are especially likely to give and receive support on social media.* Pew Research Center. Retrieved from https://www.pewresearch.org/internet/2015/07/16/parents-and-social-media/

Fielding, N. G., Lee, R. M., & Blank, G. (2017). *The SAGE Handbook of Online Research Methods* (2nd ed.). London, UK: Sage.

Hennink, M. M. (2014). *Understanding Focus Group Discussions.* New York, NY: Oxford University Press.

Krueger, R., & Casey, M. (2009). *Focus groups: A practical guide for applied research* (4th ed.). Thousand Oaks, CA: Sage.

Liamputtong, P. (2011). *Focus group methodology: Principle and practice.* Thousand Oaks, CA: Sage.

Lobe B. (2017). Best Practices for Synchronous Online Focus Groups. In R. Barbour & D. Morgan (Eds.), *A New Era in Focus Group Research* (pp. 227–250). London, UK: Palgrave Macmillan.

Mann, C., Stewart, F. (2000). *Internet communication and qualitative research: A handbook for researching online.* London, UK: Sage.

McFadden, A., Gavine, A., Renfrew, M. J., Wade, A., Buchanan, P., Taylor, J. L., Veitch, E., Rennie, A. M., Crowther, S. A., Neiman, S., & MacGillvray, S. (2017). Support for healthy breastfeeding mothers with healthy term babies. *Cochrane Database of Systematic Reviews* (2). art. no.: CD001141. Retrieved from https://discovery.ucl.ac.uk/id/eprint/1545652/1/McFadden_et_al-2017-.pdf

Medley-Rath, S. (2019). Using Facebook secret groups for qualitative data collection. *The Qualitative Report*, 24(7), 1765–1777.

Patton, M. Q. (2015). *Qualitative evaluation and research methods.* Thousand Oaks, CA: Sage.

Perrin, A., & Duggan, M. (2015). *Americans' Internet access: 200-2015: As Internet use nears saturation for some groups, a look at patterns of adoption.* Pew Research Center. Retrieved from https://www.pewresearch.org/internet/2015/06/26/americans-internet-access-2000-2015/

Poytner, R. (2010). *The handbook of online and social research.* West Sussex, UK: Wiley.

Ramo, D. E., Meacham, M., Thrul, J., Belohlavek, A., Sarkar, U., & Humfleet, G. (2019). Exploring identities and preferences for intervention among LGBTQ+ young adult smokers through online focus groups. *Journal of Adolescent Health*, 64(3), 390–397.

Reid, D. J., & Reid, F.J.M. (2005). Online focus groups: An in-depth comparison of computer-mediated and conventional focus group discussions. *International Journal of Market Research*, 47(2), 131–162.

Reisner, S. L., Randazzo, R. K., White Hughto, J. M., Peitzmeier, S., DuBois, L. Z., Pardee, D. J., Marrow, E., McLean, S., & Potter, J. (2018). Sensitive health topics with underserved patient populations: Methodological considerations for online focus group discussions. *Qualitative Health Research, 28*(10), 1658–1673.

Ripat, J., & Colatruglio, A. (2016). Exploring winter community participation among wheelchair users: An online focus group. *Occupational Therapy in Health Care, 30*(1), 95–106.

Robinson, A., Davis, M., Hall, J. N., Lauckner, C., & Anderson, A. (2019). It takes an e-village: Supporting black mothers in sustaining breastfeeding through Facebook communities. *Journal of Human Lactation, 35*(3), 569–582.

Short, S. E. (2006). Focus group interviews. In E. Perecman & S. R. Curran (Eds.), *A handbook for social science field research: Essays & bibliographic sources on research design and methods* (pp. 103–115). London, UK: Sage.

Skelton, K., Evans, R., LaChenaye, J., Amsbary, J., Wingate, M., & Talbott, L. (2018). Utilization of online focus groups to include mothers: A use-case design, reflection, and recommendations. *Digital Health, 4*, 1–6.

Stewart, D. W., & Shamdasani, P. (2015). *Focus groups: Theory and practice* (3rd ed.). Thousand Oaks, CA: Sage.

Stewart, K., & Williams, M. (2005). Researching online populations: The use of online focus groups for social research. *Qualitative Research, 5*(4), 395–416.

United States Breastfeeding Committee. (2014). *Healthy people 2020: Breastfeeding objectives.* Retrieved from http://www.usbreastfeeding.org/p/cm/ld/fid=221

Walston, J. T., & Lissitz, R. W. (2000). Computer-mediated focus groups. *Evaluation Review, 24*(5), 457–483.

Wirtz, A. L., Cooney, E. E., Chaudhry, A., & Reisner, S. L. (2019). Computer-mediated communication to facilitate synchronous online focus group discussions: Feasibility study for qualitative HIV research among transgender women across the United States. *Journal of Medical Internet Research, 21*(3).

CHAPTER EIGHT

Approaches to Support Data Analysis and Interpretations of Culturally Responsive Focus Groups

In This Chapter

- Recording Focus Group Data

- Transcription Guidelines

- Grounded Theory Strategies for Analyzing Data Generated by a Group

- Thematic Analysis of Focus Group Data

- Culturally-Anchored Focus Group Analysis and Interpretation

- Nonverbal Communication

- Computer-Assisted Analysis

THIS CHAPTER PROVIDES GUIDELINES on recording and transcribing focus group data and discusses strategies useful for culturally-centered focus group data analysis and interpretation. Some of the data analysis and interpretation techniques presented here are informed by the qualitative tradition of grounded theory (Charmaz, 2011). In addition, I present other approaches, including thematic analysis and a culturally-anchored focus group framework, advanced by Diane Hughes and Kimberly DuMont (1993). To round out the chapter, I explore nonverbal communication and computer-assisted data analysis techniques. While it is beyond the scope of this chapter to provide a detailed discussion of every recording focus group option, transcription technique, or approach to data analysis and interpretation, I aim to introduce culturally responsive inquirers to conventions that can be adopted or adapted to fit their investigations.

Recording Focus Group Data

Digital audio recorders work well to record focus group sessions, and can be placed strategically on the table close to participants, ensuring their voices are captured. Digital audio recorders have sufficient memory and can store multiple focus group sessions. Many models are USB-powered and include a USB cord to transfer your audio files onto your laptop or tablet. Smartphones are another option for recording focus group sessions. The built-in audio recording features on smartphones do a good job of recording in focus groups. To enhance sound quality, voice recorder smartphone apps are a great option. Like digital recorders, smartphones will need to be strategically placed in the focus group setting to capture all participants' voices. If the group is large, some researchers use more than one device to ensure sound quality. Specialized devices such as omnidirectional microphones are yet another option to record focus group data. Omnidirectional microphones pick up sounds from all sides of the microphone, which is ideal for focus group settings. However, while these devices result in superior sound quality, specialized microphones are costly and, depending on the situation, may not prove worth the added expense. Additional recommendations for recording focus group sessions include:

- learning and practicing the features on the recording device before conducting the focus group

- testing the device's capability to capture sound at different distances— the sound quality will be compromised if the device is too far from the speaker

- ensuring the audio device is fully charged

- locating a quiet place to conduct the focus group—some devices pick up more background noise than others

- placing the recording device on a stable surface

- storing the audio recordings in a safe and secure place

After you have recorded your focus groups, they must be transcribed. Deciding on a standard format for your transcriptions will prove invaluable for data analysis. In the following section, some guidelines for formatting focus group transcripts are discussed.

Transcription Guidelines

A focus group *transcript* is a "word-for-word written record of the focus group discussion, based on the audio recording" (Krueger & Casey, 2015, p. 150). Formats for transcripts are dependent on research questions and goals. However, there are some general recommendations for organizing transcripts. First, consistently use the same format, as this will facilitate easier examinations within and across focus group transcripts, especially when working with a research team. Next, include a labeling system. This will assist in organizing, retrieving, and analyzing the focus group data. To label a focus group transcript, include the following information:

- Name of File

- Name of Moderator

- Date of Focus Group

- Beginning Time

- Ending Time

- Name of Transcriber

- Date of Transcription

Also, include a "Comments" section as part of your transcript. This section can be placed below the labeling system and above the written account of your focus group session. This section will contain any additional information that is useful for establishing the context or making sense of the focus group data. For example, if the focus group was cut short or interrupted for some reason, that information can be placed in the Comments section. Below the Comments section, your focus group data from the audio recording is typed.

Before delving into guidelines on how to format the discussion from the focus group session, it is important to take a moment to discuss the seemingly unproblematic notion of transcribing verbatim written accounts of focus groups. As the definition of a transcript mentioned earlier indicates, the methodological literature advances the notion that a transcript reflects a word-for-word or verbatim account of the recording. However, a more critical assessment of verbatim transcription acknowledges that while a verbatim account may be the goal, a written account of the focus group session can never fully capture the audio recording nor what actually took place during the focus group session itself (Poland,1995). In addition, there is the issue of *data deterioration*—opportunities for the focus group data to be lost, altered or not even captured at all as you move from data collection to transcription (Poland, 1995). This issue is important to note, as data deterioration works against transcription quality (Poland, 1995). Data from even the most rigorously transcribed focus group will be incomplete to some extent as a result of data deterioration. The goal, then, is to maximize transcription quality by attempting to document what was said, including any nonverbal communication, as much as possible (Poland, 1995). The following sections provide transcript recommendations that attend to this goal.

The first recommendation is to bold the moderator's text. This allows you and others on your team to quickly notice who is talking. A second recommendation is to use the label "Moderator" and participants' names (pseudonyms) to further distinguish who is speaking on the written transcript. To illustrate these two recommendations, a transcript passage is provided below. It is from a focus group conducted with teachers to understand how a healthy food and beverage policy was being implemented in childcare centers.

Moderator: We had a chance to hear about some of the challenges that you face. What I want to talk about now is training. Like I mentioned before, one of our goals is to create a training program

for teachers that supports their promotion of healthy food and beverages at their childcare centers. Can you tell me about any training on nutrition you received in the past?

Shayla: It's been a while since we've had training on nutrition.

Niah: Oh, we got trained on pro solution eating healthy. You know what I'm talking about? Eating healthier (...) we just took a training on eating healthy.

Moderator: Was that something that you did online?

Niah: Yes. And I loved it. It was online. I worked at my own pace, and I don't have to listen to a lecture on the material that you get.

Another recommendation is to use transcription symbols to record pauses in the discussion or forms of interaction (i.e., laughing, overlapping talk). Common symbols applied to transcriptions have been identified in the literature (Krueger & Casey, 2015; Poland, 1995). If your research goals require a more detailed transcription, see Poland (1995) and Roulston (2010) for additional examples of transcription symbols beyond those provided in Table 8.1 *Examples of Transcription Symbols.*

The importance of transcription formatting cannot be overlooked. It plays a key role in *data management,* or the ability to organize, store, and retrieve your focus group data. Furthermore, data management sets the foundation for focus group data analysis.

Data analysis is the process that transforms raw qualitative data (in this case, focus group transcripts) to meaningful and significant findings (Patton, 2015). Data analysis is a planned and systematic process. In qualitative research, there are a variety of data analysis approaches available to researchers. However, despite the range of approaches offered in qualitative research, data analysis and interpretation of focus group data can be challenging as there is limited guidance on how to analyze data from groups (Massey, 2011). Because "grounded theory strategies can help scholars with diverse pursuits without necessarily developing a grounded theory" the fol-

Table 8.1: *Examples of Transcription Symbols*

Interaction	Symbol
Pauses	Use three consecutive dots to indicate a pause (...).
Laughing	Use parentheses for laughter (laughing).
Interruptions	Use a hyphen (-) to illustrate a focus group participant was interrupted midsentence. Example: I would like to go to the-
Overlapping talk	Use a hyphen (-) to illustrate the point at which a person's talk was disrupted, then use (overlapping) at the point where the other person's talk overlapped. Example: **Moderator: Okay, and they would like that. Is that the book?** Teacher 3: Yeah, it's called Grow- **Moderator: (overlapping) Grow it Right.**
Missing or unintelligible talk	Use (***) for missing text and (unintelligible) for talk you cannot understand.

lowing section discusses analytic techniques rooted in the grounded theory tradition (Charmaz, 2011, p. 360).

Grounded Theory Strategies for Analyzing Data Generated by a Group

Investigators who use grounded theory, an approach to inquiry initially developed by Glaser and Strauss (1967), are concerned with developing theory that is "grounded" in the data. Since its genesis, grounded theory has evolved and now includes different versions (see for example Charmaz, 2011, 2014; Corbin & Strauss, 2008, 2015). The popularity of grounded theory and its variations has persisted in the field of qualitative research in large part because its analytic strategies are highly structured and systematic. Furthermore, grounded theory strategies can be applied to projects even if the goal is not to generate theory (Charmaz, 2011). Grounded theory is culturally responsive because it can "advance understandings of how power, oppression, and inequities differentially affect individuals, groups, and categories of people" by providing analytical tools that are useful to expose connections among oppressive societal structures and the lived experiences of marginalized people (Charmaz, 2011, p. 362). One grounded theory technique used by qualitative researchers for data analysis is coding.

Coding. A *code* is a "word or short phrase that symbolically assigns a summative, salient, essence-capturing, and/or evocative attribute for a portion of language-based or visual data" (Saldaña, 2015, p. 3). To code the focus group data, the first step involves reading the transcript multiple times. The next step includes assigning a code (a word or phrase) to a section of focus group data (paragraphs, sentences, phrases). Corbin and Strauss (2015) remind us that coding is not just simply assigning a word to a piece of data; coding is a process whereby researchers assign meaning to the text (Corbin & Strauss, 2015). While interpretation will be discussed in more detail later in the chapter, at this point in the discussion I want to underscore how, during the coding process, you are determining what constitutes relevant text and assigning meaning to the text via a code. As a result, you reduce the transcript data to its most meaningful parts.

Grounded theory advances a specific approach to coding called *open coding*. This coding technique can also be described as an inductive approach to coding as open codes are "grounded" in, or derived from, the raw data rather than previous research or a review of the literature (Corbin & Strauss, 2015). Codes identified inductively, or "inductive codes," can be labeled with a name assigned by the researcher, or by applying the participant's own words as the code name. For example, referring back to the example above, after multiple readings of the teacher focus group transcript, I noticed that childcare center teachers were concerned about children's food and beverage allergies. Therefore, our team decided to create the code based on participants' concerns called "Food and Beverage Allergies."

In coding, pieces of a focus group text will be compared to other pieces of focus group text. In grounded theory, this process is called comparative analysis or the *constant comparative method* (Corbin & Strauss, 2015). As the name implies, this method requires continuous comparisons of data within and across focus group transcripts. Corbin and Strauss (2015) explain the constant comparative method this way:

> In doing constant comparisons, data are broken down into manageable pieces with each piece compared for similarities and dif-

ferences. Data that are similar in nature (referring to something conceptually similar but not necessarily a repeat of the same action or incident) are grouped under the same conceptual heading. (p. 7)

As you continue to code the raw data or transcripts, there will be occasions when the text does not match any other text in your focus group data set or corpus. This is fine, and may even signal something insightful related to the phenomenon under investigation. It is also important to note that not all the focus group text will be coded. Some text may be irrelevant; that text will not have a code assigned to it. At the same time, Yin (2011) warns that reducing the data to "manageable portions always entails the risk of ignoring some potentially insightful information because it just did not seem relevant to you at the time" (p. 186).

Once you have reviewed, compared, and coded relevant focus group text, the process of examining all the text you have labeled under a code begins. The purpose of this "within-code comparison" analytic technique is to closely examine the extent to which all the text you have labeled with that code fits together conceptually (Corbin and Strauss, 2015, p. 94). For example, as you review the text, you can assess, if, as a group, the text expresses a similar concept. A question to ask yourself as you examine your text grouping would be something like, *Does the text I have labeled for this code reflect a similar idea?* Below is an example of focus group text that was grouped within the same code to examine food and beverage allergies.

Code: Food and beverage allergies

Quote 1: *If a child is allergic to pineapples or oranges, that affects the whole center, because now we can't have that.*

Quote 2: *I'm getting more children that are having milk allergies. Yes, and so, with the* [Healthy Food and Beverage Policy], *they don't reimburse soy. No reimbursement of soy is a challenge. That's a challenge because if the doctor says that a child can only drink soy, I don't get reimbursed for buying the soy. But I got to serve the soy because that's a doctor's note saying soy.*

Within-code comparisons can result in multiple outcomes. For instance, perhaps after reviewing text under the same code, you decide that a quote or piece of data no longer fits in the group. This text may need to be abandoned or placed in a different conceptual grouping. In another case, you may view the text that you have grouped together and decide that the code label needs to be reconsidered to better capture the essence of the concept or idea. Another possibility is that after working through each code grouping, you decide that a grouping of text expresses two related but distinct ideas and, as a result, the original code grouping needs to be separated into two separate codes. Although within-coding is a time-intensive and tedious process with multiple outcomes, the process grants investigators the ability to reduce the focus group data to concepts as well as surface and distinguish various aspects of the concept or topic of interest (Corbin & Strauss, 2015). Ultimately, as you move forward with analysis, your within-code comparisons will result in "basic-level" concepts, which will be further developed into *categories* (Corbin & Strauss, 2015, p. 76). Categories are "more abstract terms that denote the major theme that a group of basic-level concepts are pointing to" (Corbin & Strauss, 2015, p. 76). After each category generated from the basic-level concept is contrasted and compared, the next step is to determine a *core category*—the most abstract category that serves to link all the other categories (and any sub-categories) together (Corbin & Strauss, 2015). Developing a core category and related categories necessitates data interpretation.

Data interpretation typically refers to how the inquirer makes sense of the data. Making sense of the data begins with "elucidating meanings" (Patton, 2015). Questioning the focus group data, as suggested by Patton (2015), is a way to closely examine and interrogate the data for explicit and implicate meanings. To elucidate meaning, Patton (2015) advises asking yourself questions such as:

- *What is happening here?*

- *What aspect of the phenomenon does this shed light on?*

- *What is missing or excluded?*

Although data interpretation is often presented in qualitative texts (including this text) as a distinct process, in practice data analysis and interpretation happen at the same time. As mentioned earlier, the coding process involves making sense of and assigning meaning to the text. While coding or analyzing your focus group data, you are making sense of the data, simultaneously fleshing out and modifying your understandings about the phenomenon as the investigation evolves. This implies interpretation is a recursive process, whereby you go back and forth, generating preliminary ideas about what is happening, applying analytic procedures (i.e., coding, categories) to closely examine what is happening, and developing refined interpretations of what is happening. This cyclical process can challenge your assumptions or preconceived ideas about the topic of interest. The process can also generate negative cases or "exceptions to the main theme or core concept of the research" (Corbin & Strauss, 2015, p. 101). Searching for negative cases enhances the interpretation of your data and "points out that life is not exact, that there are always exceptions to almost any explanation" (Corbin & Strauss, 2015, p. 101).

As culturally responsive inquirers, our goal is to produce rich interpretations *and* center stakeholders' experiences. Centering stakeholder experience involves attending to "the way participants interpret issues, the boundaries they place on definitions, and the relevance and importance they attribute to topics under discussion" (Massey, 2011, p. 23). Yet, centering stakeholders' experiences is no easy task, because, to a great extent, it relies on the inquirer's judgments (not steadfast rules) (Patton, 2015). As mentioned earlier, you, as an inquirer, decide what types of codes to use, what each code means, which pieces of text fit under a code, whether a pattern identified in the data constitutes a category or a theme, and so on. Establishing strong interpretations and centering participants' concerns are highly complex, challenging, and subjective tasks that demand inquirer reflexivity. Memos, another grounded theory technique, facilitate inquirer reflexivity and support the interpretative processes.

Memoing. This grounded theory technique involves crafting notes about what you are experiencing as a result of the research process and the data interpretation process. Although memoing has grounded theory origins, this strategy is not restricted to grounded theory. Memoing is utilized alongside other inquiry traditions and by qualitative researchers and program evaluators alike. This because the structure for writing memos is flexible. There is no wrong way to craft a memo. The style and specific purpose of the memo is the prerogative of the inquirer. Memos can be thoughtful, sloppy, incomplete, or thorough. No idea is too simple or complex. Any idea, musing, question, interpretation, feeling, concern, hunch, guess, or decision can be captured in a memo.

Of interest to culturally responsive inquirers is that memos aid reflection on the contextual characteristics (social, political, and environmental) related to the investigation. Also of interest is that memos assist with inquirer reflexivity. For this purpose, I find some of Saldaña's (2015) recommendations for memos useful. He advises using memos to reflect on your relationship with participants as well as any personal issues or ethical predicaments that occur during the study.

There are multiple advantages to using memos for data analysis and interpretation. Charmaz (2000) notes that memos help researchers to (1) systematize the analytic process, (2) grapple with ideas as they analyze the focus group data, (3) develop and refine categories, (4) clarify the relationships across categories, as well as (5) acquire greater confidence in their analysis and interpretation of the data (p. 518).

While memos can take on any style, there is a basic format for crafting memos that can increase your ability to systematize your analytic process. To format your memos, I recommend a heading with the date and a brief title related to the content of each memo you write. Doing so assists with retrieving memos, remembering what the memo was about, and modifying your thoughts later. Also, memos can serve as the foundation for your interpretations. When you have a system of memo writing in place, you can draw on them to finalize your evaluation report, article, master's thesis, or dissertation; this makes the write-up process a lot easier (Birks, Chapman, & Francis, 2008).

Analyzing the focus group data inevitably raises questions about your topic and what participants are expressing. In this regard, memos aid in sorting out your questions and cultural interpretations and support reflections on the interactions (points of disagreement) by offering a means to immerse yourself in the focus group data. Also, memos facilitate data analysis in terms of your coding process. Memos become a critical mechanism to closely examine, compare, and contrast data pieces. As you gain more clarity, your memos will reflect more in-depth understandings, fostering higher levels of analytic abstraction as relationships identified in the focus group data become more visible. By continuously interrogating your focus group data via memos, your initial assertations about what's happening (or not happening) are subject to even more scrutiny. Interrogating your focus group draws you closer, enhancing your assertions. The assertions generated from writing memos during data analysis are central to affirm (or disconfirm) your initial interpretations of concepts, events, participants' lived experiences and so on. Ultimately, interacting with the data in these ways is integral to the reflexive process and strengthens your interpretations of the focus group data. Memos are typically for your eyes only, however, if you are working with a team, memos are a mechanism to communicate your understandings to the team (Strauss & Corbin, 1998).

• To write memos, you can utilize different devices such as computers or a voice recorder (Clarke, 2005 as cited in Birks, Chapman, & Francis, 2008).

• Memos do not have to be text-based; visual devices (concept maps, charts) can illustrate and explore relationships, thoughts, meanings, processes, practices, and the sequence of events as well (Corbin & Strauss, 2015).

• Memos can assist with developing or enhancing theories (Saldaña, 2015).

So far, we have reviewed grounded theory strategies for analyzing focus group data. The following section introduces another approach to analyze focus group data, thematic analysis, an approach commonly used by qualitative researchers and program evaluators to analyze focus group data.

Thematic Analysis of Focus Group Data

Like categories, themes can be based on codes. Researchers often use *deductive coding* to develop their themes. Deductive codes derive from different sources, such as the literature related to the phenomenon of interest, theories guiding the research, research questions, or previous research studies or evaluations. Deductive codes are often established and defined before data analysis. Researchers can also use inductive codes for thematic development. Because coding often involves different types of codes, it is a highly dynamic and messy endeavor. Therefore, codebooks are used to organize and keep track of codes.

A *codebook* is not a book in the traditional sense. A codebook is a document that lists your codes and their definitions (DeCuir-Gunby, Marshall, & McCulloch, 2011). We used a codebook for our evaluation exploring how childcare centers implemented the healthy food and beverage policy. Our evaluation team decided that both deductive and inductive coding was important to our thematic analysis. We were interested in information about healthy food and beverage policy implementation that aligned with the theory (socio-ecological conceptual framework) and the quantitative data we collected during the first phase of the evaluation, as well as any information that we had not previously considered. For example, based on the theory and the survey used for our evaluation of the healthy food and beverage policy, we had several deductive or predetermined codes. One such deductive code was "Challenges." This code was used as a broad code in our codebook. Different types of challenges to implementing the policy were identified in the survey. One type of challenge was related to making water accessible to children. Therefore, we added a sub-code ("Water Concerns"), under the more general code Challenges, to the codebook prior to analysis.

As we began an inductive reading of the teacher focus group data, we noticed concerns about food and beverage allergies (discussed earlier), and difficulties with limiting the amount of highly sweetened beverages consumed by children at the childcare centers. Because the teachers' concern about sweetened beverages was a "type" of challenge, the sub-code labeled "Sweetened Beverage Intake Concerns" was added to the codebook. Another sub-code identified through our inductive analysis of the focus group data was "Encouraging Picky Eaters" (described in the theme below). An excerpt from our codebook is provided in Table 8.2 *Excerpt from Healthy Food and Beverage Policy Evaluation Codebook*, to demonstrate how the codes from our healthy food and beverage evaluation, which began with deductive codes and then expanded to include inductive codes, were organized in the codebook. As our evaluation team continued to analyze the teacher focus group data, other codes were developed, refined or even eliminated, resulting in further changes to our codebook.

You can create a codebook using whatever format works best for you and your research agenda. Some researchers use qualitative data analysis software (e.g., NVivo) for their codebook; alternatively, you could use a

Table 8.2: *Excerpt from Healthy Food and Beverage Policy Evaluation Codebook*

Code	Sub-Code	Description
Challenges	Water concerns	Descriptions related to issues (i.e., recycling, mistrust of water system, use of disposable cups, cleaning water bottles) providing water indoors or outdoors to children
	Food and beverage allergies	Descriptions about challenges related to allergies; includes their impact on policy implementation
	Sweetened beverage intake concerns	Comments related to difficulties limiting the amount of highly sweetened beverages to children
	Encouraging picky eaters	Descriptions about difficulties encouraging some children to try new healthy foods and beverages

Microsoft Word document or an Excel spreadsheet. The point here is that a thoughtful and thorough codebook supports coding and subsequent thematic analysis of the focus group data, especially when working with other coders. This is because the detailed information provided in the codebook will make it easier to conceptually distinguish between codes, thereby enabling greater consistency when coders use the codebook as a guide to assign codes to focus group data (DeCuir-Gunby, Marshall, & McCulloch, 2011).

After you have completed coding to better understand what is happening in the focus group data, the codes and related text will be closely examined to develop a *theme*. A theme is "something important about the data in relation to the research question, and represents some level of *patterned* [emphasis in original] response or meaning within the data set" (Braun & Clarke, 2006, p. 82). For instance, the code "Encouraging Picky Eaters" was further developed, resulting in the theme "Encouraging Picky Eaters to Try Something New."

Encouraging Picky Eaters to Try Something New

While many children enjoyed fruits and vegetables, teacher focus group participants discussed issues with encouraging some children to try unfamiliar foods. Specifically, this issue involves children not liking the texture of, or refusing to eat, specific fruits and vegetables. For example, teachers mentioned the challenges they face when getting children to eat food they find unappetizing. One teacher's comment illustrates this challenge:

When I first started here, she did not like baby food. She was only... like ten months. She wouldn't touch it. She would gag, and make herself throw up. To this day, she still has a thing about texture.

Another teacher reported the following challenge related to children who refuse to try new healthy foods or beverages:

Our problems are more with the picky eaters (...) the ones that just won't. And I can only do so much as an educator to be like, 'Okay, just try to eat it.' I can't physically make them open their mouth and try it. So it just makes it hard for them to be willing to try something new.

As demonstrated in the example above, a theme typically has two components: (1) a descriptive yet concise title to capture the meaning of the pattern or idea identified in the data (Salañda, 2013), and (2) relevant text or quotes that serve to illustrate that pattern or idea. While there is no cookie-cutter recipe for how to name your themes or select illustrative text, your research purpose, review of the literature, theoretical frameworks, and research questions will inform the development of your themes. As with the grouping text process, creating themes may cause you to revise your ideas, and, as a result, modify your themes. While this process is labor-intensive, developing themes permits the researcher to better comprehend the phenomenon of interest, establish connections between the focus group data and other sources (i.e., existing literature, theory, data collection methods, research questions), discover inconsistencies within and between focus groups, and transform focus group data into meaningful findings (DeCuir-Gunby, Marshall, & McCulloch, 2011; Patton, 2015).

The discussion now turns to Hughes and DuMont's (1993) culturally-anchored approach to focus group data analysis and interpretation, utilized in the context of community psychology.

Culturally-Anchored Focus Group Data Analysis and Interpretation

Because the approach offered by Hughes and DuMont (1993) stems from a framework used to analyze cultural stories (Polanyi, 1985), their culturally-anchored focus group data analysis and interpretation approach examines three forms of participant narratives. These include *descriptive statements, stories*, and *abstract generalizations*. Hughes and DuMont assert that these three narrative forms can elicit information that informs an investigator's understanding of working with culturally diverse groups. I provide a brief description of these narrative forms below; however, see Hughes and DuMont (1993) for more details.

Descriptive statements. Descriptive statements are narratives in which participants describe a set of conditions or circumstances that continue for an extended period. Descriptive statements derive from participants' responses to the researcher's focus group question. Of course, descriptive statements could also be the result of responses to other participants in the group. Hughes and DuMont (1993) note that descriptive statements typically contain singular pronouns. Data analysis here, then, centers on searching for participant statements that include pronouns such as me, she, he, mine, my, myself, and so on. Descriptive statements emphasize information about how an individual participant experiences a specific thing such as a person, event, or setting from her point of view. Coding based on the content identified in participants' descriptive statements, followed by themes illustrating how patterns compare and contrast has the potential to produce rich information.

Stories. Stories are narratives in which participants retell past events. This narrative form includes a setting and characters. Participants use stories during focus groups to "amuse, inform, illustrate, and explain perspectives that were most readily justified by way of concrete examples" (Hughes & DuMont, 1993, p. 793). Stories can be directly prompted by a focus group question or simply emerge. Whatever the case, the point is to look for instances when participants describe a sequence of events when examining the focus group data. Once you've identified a story in the data, you can use inductive coding and further analyze the segments of the story for content. However, it's not just the story that is worthy of analysis. Also, of interest when analyzing a story is the group's response to the story. Hughes and DuMont (1993) clarify the aspects of analyzing a story when they state the story serves as the impetus or "stimulus that prompts participants to interpret their experiences within the context of the other group members" (p. 795). This means you want to pay close attention to how participants react after hearing the story. Do they all agree with the story? Do they disagree with the story?

As Onwuegbuzie, Dickinson, Leech, and Zoran (2009) rightly argue, when interpreting focus group data, excluding information about the extent to which participants agreed or disagreed, results in "dissenters effectively being censored or marginalized" (p. 5). Including information about dissenters, in particular, contributes to the descriptiveness of the topic under investigation (Onwuegbuzie, Dickinson, Leech, & Zoran, 2009). If working with a marginalized group, including the voices of dissenters would be especially critical, so as not to further marginalize participants. In short, how participants respond to the story indicates how they interpret its meaning, which, in turn, produces fruitful insights into the groups' cultural experience and a strong foundation for culturally sensitive interpretations.

Abstract generalizations. Abstract generalizations are "summary statements describing principles that participants have extracted from their own and other group members' common experiences"; these narratives include plural pronouns such as them, they, their, we, and our (Hughes & DuMont, 1993, p. 795). Abstract generalizations describe how the group perceives its position in society relative to other groups. That is, this type of narrative emphasizes "intergroup relations" (Hughs & DuMont, 1993, p. 796). In contrast to participants' uses of a story format to illustrate particular events, they often use abstract generalizations to index their broader worldviews or how the "world works" from their unique standpoints.

Nonverbal Communication

The ability to observe interactions between participants is a key advantage of focus groups. Interactions include nonverbal communication such as body movements (i.e., gestures, facial expressions), tone of talk (i.e., emotional), as well as talk interactions (i.e., pauses). However, as Denham and Onwuegbuzie (2013) argue, investigators do not pay enough attention to nonverbal communication when analyzing data. Why do qualitative researchers pay insufficient attention to nonverbal communication? Based on their review of qualitative research textbooks and course syllabi, Denham and Onwuegbuzie (2013) assert that verbal and written communication is privileged by Western researchers. Glenn (2004) elaborates on this point by asserting that in Western culture, "speaking or speaking out continues to signal power, liberation, culture, or civilization itself" (p. 3 as cited in Kawabata & Gastaldo, 2015). Yet, privileging verbal communication is not sensitive to other cultures that rely on and value forms of nonverbal communication. For example, Kawabata and Gastaldo (2015) discuss how people in Japan use "indirect and ambiguous" communication strategies, namely silence, as a way to maintain unity within their communities (p. 6). Furthermore, these researchers rightly argue, "cultural indifference toward silence [nonverbal communications] not only inhibits researcher's abilities to construct meaningful accounts but also negatively influences research outcomes" (Kawabata & Gastaldo, 2015, p. 1).

To advance the importance of nonverbal forms of communication, Denham and Onwuegbuzie (2013) identified numerous benefits of analyzing nonverbal communication data alongside focus group narratives. They suggest that nonverbal communication is valuable to:

- corroborate narratives.

- capture underlying messages.

- discover nonverbal behaviors that contradict the narratives.

- broaden understanding of the phenomena of interest.

- create new directions based on additional insights.

Denham and Onwuegbuzie (2013) also offer a typology of codes, building from Saldaña's (2012) coding typology to code nonverbal communication data. These codes include: *corroborate coding, capture coding, discover coding, broaden coding,* and new *directions coding.* Denham and Onwuegbuzie (2013) posit that the use of their coding typology is "not as important as what the codes involve—namely, the intersection of verbal and nonverbal data" (p. 12). That is, establishing a process for analyzing nonverbal communication to inform the data analysis of narratives is important as it will yield more robust understandings than analyzing narratives alone (Denham & Onwuegbuzie, 2013).

Computer-Assisted Analysis

Krueger and Casey (2015) discuss multiples ways that computers can assist with the analysis strategies described above, among others. You can, for example, cut and paste the selected text into their code groupings using a Word document. While this method allows you to group text and notice patterns within and across groupings of text and themes, it is difficult to reference back to the quote source. To assist with this, Krueger and Casey (2015) recommend devising a color-coding system or some other system to keep track of text sources.

Another way is to use an Excel spreadsheet to code your focus group data. Like the first approach, the advantage of this one is that it allows you to use computer software that most researchers have at their disposal. However, Krueger and Casey (2015) note this approach to analysis is a bit more cumbersome and less "powerful" relative to software designed for qualitative data analysis (p.156).

The third approach to computer-assisted focus group data analysis is the use of qualitative data analysis software (QDAS). QDAS programs are intentionally designed for qualitative research, and have increased in popularity and recognition amongst qualitative researchers and evaluators. More and more scholars (primarily from the United Kingdom, United States, Netherlands, Canada, and Australia) in a variety of disciplinary areas are using QDAS, primarily NVivo and Atlas.ti (Woods, Paulus, Atkins, & Macklin, 2016). QDAS programs are compatible with many inquiry designs and analytic approaches, such as the ones described in this chapter. Scholars are using QDAS for the analysis of focus group data, as well as other data sources including individual interviews, documents, observation field notes and open-ended survey questions (Woods et al., 2016). A QDAS program has many capabilities. For instance, it gives you the capacity to easily create and manage (reorganize, merge, remove) your codes, keep track of where your text or quotes came from, craft memos, and develop a codebook. QDAS programs also offer you the ability to conduct advanced data analysis techniques such as visualizing (graphs, charts) how codes are related to each other and comparing codes generated by different researchers. However, QDAS programs do not actually conduct the analysis (Bazeley, 2012; Kikooma, 2010)—the researcher is still required to analyze the content as well as attend to the culture and context related to the project.

Furthermore, there are some concerns related to using QDAS programs. The first relates to researchers' analyzing data based on the features offered by the QDAS program, rather than using a more reflexive approach to analysis informed by the overarching design (i.e., case study, ethnography) and relevant theories (Woods et al., 2016). Another concern is the amount of time it takes for researchers to learn how to use the software features (Woods et al., 2016; Zamawe, 2015). In addition, it can take a significant amount of time for researchers to integrate QDAS into their inquiry practices and report their usage of QDAS tools in their research (Woods et al., 2016). That said, QDAS programs can systematize significant amounts of data, make data retrieval easier, and make data analysis more transparent (Woods et al., 2016).

Summary

In this chapter, I have discussed how recordings and transcripts are merely representations of the focus group experience and not the experience itself. I also highlighted the impact of data deterioration on data quality, and offered strategies to enhance focus group recording and transcription quality. I also outlined grounded theory analytic strategies and thematic analysis, as well as a culturally-anchored approach to responsively and systematically analyze and interpret focus groups. These approaches illuminate the processes that assist researchers with the development of their cultural interpretations.

References

Bazeley, P. (2012). Regulating qualitative coding using QDAS? *Sociological Methodology, 42*(1), 77–78.

Birks, M., Chapman, Y., & Francis, K. (2008). Memoing in qualitative research: Probing data and processes. *Journal of Research in Nursing, 13*(1), 68–75.

Braun, V., & Clarke, V. (2006). Using thematic analysis in psychology. *Qualitative Research in Psychology, 3*(2), 77–101.

Charmaz, K. (2011). Grounded theory methods in social justice research. In N. K. Denzin & Y. Lincoln (Eds.), *Handbook of qualitative research* (4th ed.) (pp. 359–380). Thousand Oaks, CA: Sage.

Charmaz, K. (2014). *Constructing grounded theory.* Thousand Oaks, CA: Sage.

Corbin, J., & Strauss, A. (2008). *Basics of qualitative research: Techniques and procedures for developing grounded theory* (3rd ed.). Thousand Oaks, CA: Sage.

Corbin, J., & Strauss, A. (2015). *Basics of qualitative research: Techniques and procedures for developing grounded theory* (4th ed.). Thousand Oaks, CA: Sage.

Clarke, A. (2005). *Situational analysis: Grounded theory after the postmodern turn.* Thousand Oaks, CA: Sage.

DeCuir-Gunby, J. T., Marshall, P. L., & McCulloch, A. W. (2011). Developing and using a codebook for the analysis of interview data: An example from a professional development research project. *Field Methods, 23*(2), 136–155.

Denham, M. A., & Onwuegbuzie, A. J. (2013). Beyond words: Using nonverbal communication data in research to enhance thick description and interpretation. *International Journal of Qualitative Methods, 12*(1), 670–696.

Glaser, B., & Strauss, A. (1967). *The discovery of grounded theory strategies for qualitative research.* Mill Valley, CA: Sociology Press.

Hughes, D. L., & DuMont, K. (1993). Using focus groups to facilitate culturally anchored research. *American Journal of Community Psychology, 21*(6), 775–806.

Kawabata, M., & Gastaldo, D. (2015). The less said, the better: Interpreting silence in qualitative research. *International Journal of Qualitative Methods, 14*(4), 1–9.

Kikooma, J. (2010). Using qualitative data analysis software in a social constructionist study of entrepreneurship. *Qualitative Research Journal, 10*(1), 40–51.

Krueger, R. A. & Casey, M. A. (2015). *Focus groups: A practical guide for applied research* (5th ed.). Thousand Oaks, CA: Sage.

Massey, O. T. (2011). A proposed model for the analysis and interpretation of focus groups in evaluation research. *Evaluation and program planning, 34*(1), 21–28.

Onwuegbuzie, A. J., Dickinson, W. B., Leech, N. L., & Zoran, A. G. (2009). A qualitative framework for collecting and analyzing data in focus group research. *International Journal of Qualitative Methods, 8*(3), 1–21.

Patton, M. Q. (2015). *Qualitative evaluation and research methods.* Thousand Oaks, CA: Sage.

Poland, B. D. (1995). Transcription quality as an aspect of rigor in qualitative research. *Qualitative Inquiry, 1*(3), 290–310.

Saldaña, J. (2015). *The coding manual for qualitative researchers.* Thousand Oaks, CA: Sage.

Woods, M., Paulus, T., Atkins, D. P., & Macklin, R. (2016). Advancing qualitative research using qualitative data analysis software (QDAS)? Reviewing potential versus practice in published studies using ATLAS.ti and NVivo, 1994–2013. *Social Science Computer Review, 34*(5), 597–617.

Yin, R. K. (2011). *Applications of case study research.* Thousand Oaks, CA: Sage.

Sample Focus Group Protocol

Welcome

Thank you for allowing me to talk with you. My name is Jori Hall and I'm the moderator for today's focus group session. Today is a chance for you to share your Professional Development School (PDS) experiences. As this project proceeds, I will meet with other stakeholders to explore their PDS experiences as well. The purpose of this research is to document how PDS activities are enacted and experienced so that each PDS stakeholder group can learn from the other and to enhance the district-wide mission of the PDS.

Ground rules

Before we get started, I would like to remind you that the consent form you signed acknowledges that your answers are confidential. If I ask any questions that you would rather not answer, feel free to say so and I will gladly move on to a different question. The interview should take about 45 minutes and will be audio recorded. You will need to turn off all mobile devices/phones. Also, please speak one at a time and in a clear voice. Do you have any questions before we begin?

Topic: General PDS context and goals

To begin, I would like to get your general impressions regarding how the school is functioning as a PDS.

1. In general, how are things going at the school?

2. Focusing exercise: On a scale of one to ten, with ten being the best, how would you rate the school as a PDS?

    a. PROBE: Why not a higher number? Why not a lower number?

Topic: professional development of PDS school and UGA faculty

Central to a PDS is the professional development it provides to teachers and teacher candidates. Now, I would like you to reflect on a successful professional development experience you had since working at this school.

3. Please describe this experience. Share why you think it was most successful.

    a. PROBE: Who was involved? In what ways, if any, did it impact your classroom practice?

Topic: inquiry directed at the improvement of practice

Next, I would like to ask about any experiences that you've had with research at the school.

4. Please describe any research activities that you led or co-facilitated (with university faculty or other teachers) at the school?

    a. PROBE: If teachers have not conducted research at the school, then ask teachers to share some reasons for this. If so, then ask: From your perspective, what was accomplished by conducting this research?

Topic: enhanced student learning

At this point, I would like to ask some questions about how the PDS model at the school enhances student learning.

5. In your opinion, what are the top three practices (or initiatives) of this

particular PDS model that most enhances student learning?

6. What is most helpful to support these practices/initiatives?

7. If the federal government were going to give this PDS a grant for $100,000, what would you recommend the school administrators do with the money?

Topic: Organizational culture and climate

The last part of our discussion focuses on the culture and climate of the PDS.

8. If an administrator from a non-PDS visited this school and asked you to characterize your PDS, what would you say? Put differently, what makes your PDS model distinct?

a. PROBE: Do you believe these distinctions are related to the school being a PDS? When thinking about the current school year, what distinctive school practice or procedure comes to mind?

9. How would you describe the overall culture and climate at the school?

   a. PROBE: How do you feel when you walk into the building each day? How might a student (parent, or community member) describe walking into this school building?

Closing

I greatly appreciate your taking time to talk with me and share your PDS experiences. Is there anything else that you would like to share that we have not covered?

Using Sista Circles to Conduct Research About and With Sista Scholars

Using Sista Circles to Conduct Research About and With Sista Scholars

by Lemesha C. Brown, PhD

Sista circles were utilized to explore the experiences of first-generation Black women attending graduate school and what contributed to their persistence. The study took place at a large, public, predominantly White institution in the Southeast region of the United States. To guide the research study, I used Community Cultural Wealth (CCW) (Yosso, 2005) and Black feminist thought (BFT) (Collins, 2000). CCW and BFT are theories with a critical lens that recognize how structures serve to oppress people with minoritized identities. CCW centers Communities of Color, from an asset-based perspective, and their multiple forms of capital in educational settings. BFT focuses on the multiple identities that Black women hold and how those identities intersect to create very nuanced experiences for Black women. CCW and BFT were relevant because they allowed me to identify the ways that my sista scholars experienced their doctoral programs differently based on their multiple identities and what capital they utilized to persist through despite those experiences.

Sista circles are culturally responsive in that they incorporate the ways in which Black women are, communicate, and make meaning together. Because these features value Black women and their interactions, sista circle methodology was deemed appropriate for this study. Sista circles were my main method for data collection. As the researcher, I not only facilitated the discussion, I also participated in the dialogue. Also, having an individual to serve as a note taker of the interactions and emotions of the group was essential.

Along with identifying as first-generation, Black, and women, my sista scholars were at least in their second semester of their doctoral programs. Six sista scholars from different academic disciplines participated in three sista circles. The sista circles took place at my home, which added a level of familiarity, bringing comfort to the process. Each week, I cooked a meal that we could enjoy as a group. The sista scholars could arrive up to one hour before our circle started to eat dinner. The first week, we were able to talk and get to know each other a little more before we started the circle. Each week after was used to check in and catch up with each other prior to beginning our sista circle session. Cooking and offering food was a means for me to connect and build rapport with my sista scholars. Additionally, being able to "break bread" with one another allowed the sista scholars to speak with the other women in the group more informally before getting into the topics each evening. Furthermore, because sista circle methodology recognizes Black women as more than just participants, I referred to the women in the focus groups as "sista scholars." Sista circle methodology also recognizes power differentials inherent in the research process, despite any characteristics shared between the researcher and sistas in the group—in this case we were all Black women pursuing our graduate degrees at the time the study was conducted. Therefore, referring to participants as sista scholars was also useful to decrease power differentials.

There were four major findings within my research study. First, it was evident from all of our experiences that being in a doctoral program resulted in various physical and mental health concerns including but not limited to weight gain, disordered eating, and anxiety. Second, as first-generation students, the sista scholars felt they often did not know how to navigate their respective doctoral programs. Third, sista scholars' perceived their social class as negatively impacting their doctoral education, as they often had multiple jobs that took time away from their studies, for example. And the fourth finding revealed strategies utilized by sista scholars to persevere through the ups and downs that come with doctoral education. One notable strategy was relying on their personal networks (i.e., family and friends). These findings will be disseminated via academic journals. For greater accessibility, the findings will also be distributed via social media.

Lessons Learned

As a result of conducting sista cirlces, a few lessons were learned. First, I learned how the ability to come together over a meal was valuable to informally start building rapport, which laid the foundation needed to support my role as participant-researcher. Second, I noticed that I over-prepared for the first circle, which caused it to go longer than planned. After reflecting on this, in the remaining sista circles I made sure to ask fewer questions to ensure multiple voices were heard. Third, I realized the challenges of the participant-researcher role. For example, this role may cause you to drive the conversation, which has implications for data analysis and interpretation. Hence, conversations with your note taker and member checking with sista focus group members becomes especially critical. Last, it is also important to recognize that while you may share the same identity (i.e., Black woman), your experiences are not the same. We have multiple privileged and marginalized identities that impact our everyday experiences.

If planning to use sista circles, you, as a researcher must be willing to be vulnerable in the process, which is in contrast to more traditional approaches to research. Just as my sista scholars shared, I too shared. However, being vulnerable also has ethical implications for your relationship with participants. Therefore, you will want to critically consider how to employ sista circles in ways that respect and protect you, as the researcher, as well as your sista participants.

JORI N. HALL is an interdisciplinary scholar and research methodologist. Her scholarship broadly focuses on culturally responsive inquiry. Within the domain of culturally responsive inquiry, her research centers on values-engagement and educative approaches to evaluation, which is informed by her qualitative and mixed methods work. Her approaches to inquiry are primarily concerned with how programs and policies engage participants' values responsibly, the educative potential of evaluation theory and practice, and enhancing the overall quality and credibility of social science research and evaluation. She has numerous peer-reviewed articles and book chapters in edited volumes, handbooks, and journals related to formative evaluation methodologies, the role of values in evaluation, and mixed methods theory and practice. Hall has over a decade of experience teaching courses on evaluation and qualitative research theory and design, and mixed methods approaches to social science. As a program evaluator, she provides consultations and evaluation services for programs in various contexts, and is currently an associate editor for the *American Journal of Evaluation*. Hall received her doctorate in Educational Policy Studies from the University of Illinois at Urbana-Champaign; currently, she is an associate professor in the Qualitative Research Program at the University of Georgia.

INDEX